'Love and Mood'
by
Federico Leso

(The Theory of Mood)

Contents

Love: The Myth

(The § symbol indicates a friend talking)

§ It's nice to wake up in the morning and be happy, delighted, relaxed.

It's great to wake up with the desire to smile at everything that surrounds you: people, things and the whole world.

It's amazing to think that you're about to live a new day, and that you'll experience it and love it.

I'm happy, I love the world and its people. Life is a magnificent adventure, but I needed to realise it is a divine gift, I needed to discover it and I've been lucky because you've come into my life… And brought love with you.

True love, that which I've hoped and dreamed for, that which restores our faith in everything and everyone, that which is absolute and above all things.

The day we met was a day like any other; our meeting was unexpected, but it happened because we were both looking for the same thing and we found it together. Was fate or perhaps luck, who knows? What matters is that this wonderful thing called love had finally made its debut.

How much I believe in it! How much I want you! How much I love you!

With love, I have again found tranquillity,

happiness, meaning in every day, indeed of life itself. With love, I have again found peace, hope and the will to live.

Emotions, thoughts, and dreams: everything is stronger, more alive, and more intense. With you, I have found joy, inner balance and peace. This, and only this, is what one ought to seek in life.

You are my all, you are everything to me. I want only you. Nothing else matters.

You make me feel good, you make me happy; love is well-being, love is happiness, love is everything.

***

My dear…

Your eyes are drops of dew

Your hair is a crop of golden wheat

Your smile is love and joy

And your words are music and poetry…

Love: The Friend

How cool you are: you fell in love! You finally found your soulmate; you found love and thus a faithful partner for life. Well done, I'm really happy for you!

I must say that your castle is so nice. It's up there, in the air, flying free, and it's a pleasure to admire it from down here. Woe to anyone who touches it, right? I'm warning you! Woe to anyone who sets it creaking or even causes it to collapse! Why would someone destroy such a beautiful work of art? It would be a real crime, a sacrilege!

Have you ever been inside this castle, though?

§ No way. It's up there above the clouds. How does one even do that? How can I even get there? I'm not a bird! But it's up there and it exists, and I'm happy and content as I am. Why are you asking me all these questions? Is there a problem?

Absolutely not. It's really great, I confirm that. Let me offer you my most sincere congratulations and best wishes. You can rest assured that I'll not touch your castle, also because there's no need: it'll do everything by itself. You just have to wait a bit…

§ Ah… You're very funny. A true friend. You say that because you're a little envious, aren't you? A little jealous?

For goodness' sake, don't talk like that! And come on, let's face it: even if it were to collapse, and unfortunately it's going to happen sooner or later, you can always build a new one, and then a new one …. Life goes on, you know; history never changes but repeats itself. I'm sorry, I didn't mean to offend you.

Of course, I also agree that it's awesome to be in love, to love a woman and to care for her; in short, to feel a boundless love for your partner. It's the easiest and most natural way to be happy, relaxed and to live well. As if by magic, when you're in love, you create a shield against all of life's problems: everything looks better and everyone seems nicer. When you're in love, even the worst films or songs don't seem so bad. Of course, you have to be lucky, don't you think?

§ Lucky in what way?

Well, to find the right person. By the way, have you ever wondered if the right person exists? If luck exists?

§ Of course it does! You just need to look for it!

Do you mean luck or the right person?

§ The right person, of course. You are kind of annoying me, so let's get this pointless and shallow conversation over with.

You're right, I'm sorry, but now sit and just hear

me talk about luck and the right person. There are billions of women in the world, but we can't meet or experience all of them. I wish we could! Let's say that we meet a few of them, at best, and then we make a choice. Is that how it works?

§ Yes, it should be so. We obviously cannot meet all of them; let's say that we, indeed, meet a reasonable number of them and then we choose the best for us.

That's the theory and that's how it should work, but I can assure you that reality is somewhat different: there's often a chance encounter, then something clicks, like a roof tile falling on you, and from there, without choices or reasoning, your mythical castle is built. That's reality! Forget any careful selection of your partner.

§ Well, come to think of it, I must admit that it may happen. Actually, that's what happened to me.

Maybe it really takes a little luck … To find the right person, I mean. I've been really lucky to meet my beloved because she's the perfect person for me and I am the same for her. She's my better half, and together we complete each other. I have no doubt about this…

… And you'll not make me change my mind!

Clarification

1) The term 'love' used in this book has two meanings: real, concrete and universal love, and love meant as the first part of a couple's relationship. They are two very different things but I use the same term, as everyone usually does anyway. There should be no overlap between them at any given time: context will clarify the correct meaning.

2) The presence of children is not necessary to define a '**family**'. Over the years (usually two), a couple can become a family too, with the same privileges and, most importantly, the same responsibilities!

Love: Doubts

It's good to be in love, we all agree with that. What could be more wonderful than falling in love, dreaming, flying high, being happy and in sync with one's partner? It's amazing. This kind of love is grand, unconditional, awesome. It is the reason why we are born, and indeed it may be the most important reason for our existence, and it is surely the thing that, more than anything else, makes us feel better, improves our mood, and makes us happy.

Love is **everywhere**: we find it in poems, novels, songs and films, in every age and place on our incredible planet. This is the irrefutable evidence of the importance and immense power it has for us small, helpless beings. Who can deny it?

It's impossible to disagree or to challenge a truth so clear and obvious. Only a fool or a madman would do that. It's like this for everybody: love is our greatest dream, our most important myth.

Think of all the artists, writers, poets and songwriters who have delighted in this subject and managed to create all the magnificent masterpieces that brighten our days ... Surely they didn't make a huge mistake or simply waste their time?

Are we kidding? They are the best of humanity, the greatest minds who give of their creative best every day to create superlative works of arts that enable us to dream and live more fully. We can only thank them, trusting them and their art blindly, not accuse them of wasting time!

Thus, a love relationship is the best, dearest, most concrete and fundamental thing in our lives. Everything else is subordinate, incidental.

Right, we are all happy to agree, and that's great.

Is it really right, though? Is it really true?

If only it were! Unfortunately, it isn't, I'm sorry to say. This isn't reality: it would be too easy. Reality is something else altogether.

Of course, I'm happy and content, but … when it comes to love, there are also many unanswered questions and problem.

What is it after all that troubles the our romantic dreams and disturbs our joyful and untiring search for love? An infinite number of doubts that requires an infinite number of answers.

We are suspended in a limbo which we obviously don't really understand. At least, I don't. If you don't have any doubts and are sure about everything, then…

… Just cast the first stone!

Love: Conflict

Sadly, it is clear that something *does* exist that disrupts romantic love; regrettably there is something that clashes with this fabulous world, with this magnificent universe of sense and thought. It's only a small thing, but it isn't easy to push it away or ignore it. Let's say that at best we can gracefully hold it at bay for a certain amount of time; in the long run, however, this is not sustainable. This little thing is called '**reality**'.

Let's analyse love in it's two distinct parts: the real and concrete part, less visible and less loved by its user, and the part made of dreams and fantasies. This is the part that dominates, and it's usually the part everyone is in search of.

§ Don't these two parts go well together? Are they compatible?

I would say yes, at least at the beginning of the relationship, as they don't cause particular problems in the short term; but over time, they inexorably conflict with each another; it's inevitable, and we find ourselves right in the middle of these two forces, practically between the hammer and the anvil. It's a free-for-all!

§ Sorry, but can't we choose a side? Can't we choose one, excluding the other, in order not to create unnecessary conflicts?

I take the myth, please, as it makes me feel much better; actually, I'll take two of them, because you never know! Reality? No, thanks, you can have it. I'm more than happy to leave it to you. My best wishes! Brrrr … I shudder at the very thought! Who the hell invented that annoying killjoy that destroys our dreams and our love?

Right, maybe we shouldn't think about it, nor look at it; just turn around and pretend it doesn't exist. We humans, indeed, are masters of pretending, but then the chickens come home to roost, anyway. Inevitably, we have to deal with reality, if we want our relationships to survive.

'Infinite love, magnificent and above all else. You and I, my dear, are one single thing till death do us part.'

This is the myth, this is the dream, this is the art of loving; but this isn't reality, this isn't the truth. If only! If that were the case, couples would have no problem or conflict and there wouldn't be any break ups or separations. Unfortunately, reality is quite different.

A couple's love is never eternal. With time, doubts, hesitations and uncertainties build up and love wanes. Pleasant emotions, comfort, harmony and any desire to live together decrease; everything changes and nothing is ever the same as it was before.

If it is true love, I wonder, why should it change? Why should it dry up with the passing of time? It doesn't make sense. It's illogical. By definition, love is stronger than anything and nothing should be able to undermine it.

Then, why do partners desire their lives back at some point? Why do they want a new lover? Why do they break up? Why does the number of separations equal the number of marriages? What has became of love?

It is said love is over. Some tightrope walkers even make a larger claim: 'Love has changed; it's more mature and better now!'

If that's true, then why are couples less happy? And all this as if it were something normal, a tolerable and physiological accident or evolutionary inevitability. Love that's born and then dies, or simply changes.

To quote: '... love itself will evolve into family, acquiring new importance and amplifying its role.'

Ha, ha, ha! What nonsense! Who could have written such a thing?

I'll be damned, love can neither end nor change, that is not possible. Love is love: strong, loyal, invincible, above all else and forever. Love can't be vague, finite or have an expiration date like milk. Love must stand on solid ground, on a strong and steady foundation; it certainly cannot be a castle flying freely in the air...

§ All right, smart guy, genie of the lamp, stop for a moment! What do you mean by all this? That you have doubts about the existence of romantic love, perhaps? Ha, ha, ha, you're hilarious.

You said yourself how many poems, novels, films and songs demonstrate that love is true and concrete. They are official documents, kid, and they have been around for centuries of human history! You don't think you can deny all of them?

A couple's love exists, it's obvious, and it will always exist. Its solid foundation is set firmly on the ground. Forget flying castles and clouds, as you say! Love is magnificent, majestic, an unstoppable force. Nothings is more powerful, greater or truer. Love is real, concrete, crystal clear and perfect.

This is love, and this is what makes us happy, brings us together and enables us live together in peace and harmony!

Well, I didn't really say any of this, you said it. What I mean, let me say it again, is that none of this holds water, it can't last. Come on, we've all been there and we are well aware of how every love story ends. It is enough to listen to any conversation between two lovers to measure the strength their love still has.

'But then don't you love me? You do. Really? How much?'

'Are you sure? Do you finally understand? Was it useful to take a break? How much time do you still need?'

'I thought the love between us had died… Maybe not, maybe yes, I don't know… Really… It depends on the day.'

'I can't live without you… But I can't live with you either!'

'Now I know what I want: I want you… or maybe I want someone else. I want both; actually, I want all three. Ah!'

It's clear that this argument is blurred, fanciful and uncertain, but love is never blurred, it is never fanciful and much less uncertain.

§ You're insane. You're creating problems that don't exist.

Problems that don't exist? Do you mean that problems between lovers don't exist?

The fact is that history repeats itself and in the same way for everybody: love starts at full throttle, takes off, flies high above the clouds; after a while, though, it inevitably loses height and falls. That's when a thousand doubts and a thousand questions come into play, followed by a thousand fleeting answers.

Love is real and exists, but it seems that love between two lovers doesn't reflect its peculiar and highly praised 'organoleptic' characteristics; actually, it doesn't seem easily digestible…

… Without the help of a good digestive!

Definition of Love

Love: an intense feeling of affection, solidarity, empathy, charity, benevolence and generosity toward someone or something. It's wanting someone else's happiness, giving without asking, etc.

Love in a relationship, therefore, means desiring what's best for the other person, wanting their happiness, helping and comforting them, and all of that without asking for anything in return. In other words, a true act of Christian charity.

'I'm with you, my love, because I want you to be happy. I want to protect you from everything and everyone, and I do it for free, without thought of profit.'

This and this alone is what love between two lovers is, and should be. It's a noble sentiment and a source of pride for humankind.

If all this is true, how much generosity, altruism and kindness there is in the world.

Rivers of words, miles of film, novels, poems, songs, movies, all describing and telling the story about human kindness and generosity. How incredible!

I never thought that the world was so full of love and magnanimous and charitable people. I had never noticed before. I must be blind, I guess. This all gives me great joy and peace of mind.

Then, I'm magnanimous and charitable too. I'm almost a saint and never saw it coming.

… Love is great, so are the world and its people.

Crime News (Part One)

Unfortunately, almost every day newspapers and TV shows make us aware of all the tragic news about relationship dynamics. We learn of people that commit illogical acts of violence, even going so far as to kill themselves or someone else, out of love. They put an end to their lives, destroy themselves or others, and they do it out of love toward their partner.

These behaviour patterns are beyond comprehension because you can't link love and violence. It's unsustainable and cannot be condoned by anyone.

By definition, love means to give without asking, to wish for someone else's happiness; love as an act of charity and full generosity. Instead, in those cases, people want their partner to suffer or, even worse, to die. It can't be explained in the context of love.

If someone loves someone else, they can't possibly hurt them just because they got dumped.

People that commit extreme acts of violence are surely in a state of deep psychological suffering; indeed, no one who is well would do something like that. Suffering is a necessary condition for this tragic act, whatever it is.

It seems love itself is the major cause of this immense suffering and of the subsequent act of violence.

That can't be true, though: suffering out of love can't be real. With love you get happiness, joy and serenity. Love can never be the cause of suffering and if anything, it mitigates pain.

The tragic act can have two purposes: to soothe suffering, directly eradicating the alleged cause, and to make the partner suffer, in a sort of cruel revenge.

Love and revenge: those two words clash too. They are incompatible, which means that one of them is wrong!

Could the word 'love' be the wrong one? Maybe, but if love exists between two partners, then all of this is neither justifiable nor acceptable. This is the sad reality that repeats itself again and again almost every day…

§ You don't understand anything. Is this really the sum of it? It's true, I admit it, these things happen. You just need to read a newspaper to come across them. Yet, you can't put everything in one basket! One swallow doesn't make a summer! How many millions of couples are there in the world and nothing untoward ever happens to them, where love triumphs? It's true, there is a small minority of couples where there is no evidence of love, but only hate and violence, and they are different. They are the exception that proves the universal rule of romantic love. End of discussion!

It's true, you're right when you say that they are rare, that they are extreme acts and that the media evidently magnify the phenomenon. Are you sure, though, that those couples are so different? That it isn't just the extreme manifestation of a common phenomenon?

These are blatant acts of violence, acts devoid of love, which you see and hear about. However, there are also acts of violence that are totally silent and that that no one barely notices; no one dies because of them, but they too are devoid of love. Does the exception not prove the rule? Thus, on the whole, love may not be prevalent in most relationships; it may even be completely absent.

Let's go back to crime news, making two plausible examples:

1) A man and a woman break up, but he can't accept it. He suffers, argues with her and commits an extreme gesture, killing her.

2) The same lovers break up, but she can't accept it. She suffers and commits an extreme gesture, killing herself. She leaves a note: 'I killed myself out of our love.'

No! Stop! It can't be like that. They are not acts of love, nor acts dictated by a heart full of love; they are extreme responses, caused by tremendous suffering.

All this demonstrates is that love may not be the only force that binds two people together. Something else is at stake, something equally strong and intense, something linked to the measure of human suffering.

§ If it isn't love that unites two people, partially or completely, what does?

We can't exclude love *a priori*. Of course, we can say that even love has a right to exist, somehow, but the fact is that it may not prevail, nor even be the true reason why a couple gets together in the first place and nor therefore of their subsequent separation. This non-prevalence, and thus related weakness, is caused by the presence of something even stronger than love; so strong that it can hide, annihilate or override it…

… What's the name of such a mysterious thing?

Pain and Pleasure

Physical pain exists. Everybody knows and feels pain. It's an indispensable function of the body enabling the survival of all animal species, including ourselves. This function is meant to **guide our behaviour** and our actions, for the purpose of protecting us from the dangers surrounding us.

Unless we are pathologically ill, we never do anything that causes ourselves harm, or at least we try not to; this way, we defend our physical integrity and indeed, our own survival and that of our species.

While it's true, we don't do anything to hurt ourselves, at the same time it's also true that we willingly do things that give us pleasure. It's simply the other side of the same coin. Pleasure, like pain, is a function that is meant to guide our actions: pain to discourage negative behaviour patterns, pleasure to encourage positive and useful ones.

Now let's try to consider these two functions as one function (pain-pleasure) and represent them on a graph: the x-axis represents the passage of time, while the y-axis represents the level of pain or pleasure we feel, as represented by a number. We could suppose that six and up are the progressive levels of pleasure, while five and down are the progressive levels of pain.

Let's give an example from everyday life: one morning we wake up with a stomach-ache and throughout the day we think about what we ate the previous evening. Then, at the end of the day, we take a warm bath, in order to unwind and recover a sense of mental and physical well-being.

A hammer blow on a finger could be considered a great example too! Anyway, this is what the graph would probably look like:

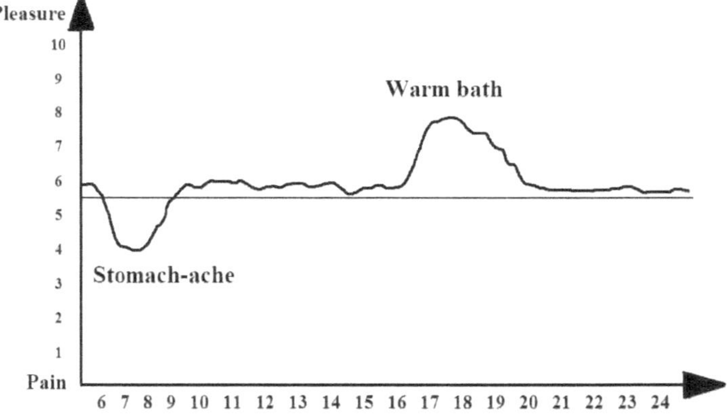

This is an innate function; thus, it's genetically determined, but it can be changed by experience. In fact, the environment or any situation that makes us go through specific experiences of pain or pleasure can modify the subsequent functions in an important way, both in a positive and in a negative sense.

Physical pain, alas, is not alone. Unfortunately, it isn't the only cause of human suffering, because you don't only suffer physically but also mentally.

Thus, we must distinguish between physical pain and another kind of pain: deep, mental anguish, pain of the soul and thus of our psyche. We might call it 'psychological' pain and its counterpart could be called 'psychological' pleasure.

If we put those two functions together, as we did with the physical functions, we find a single function that represents nothing more than our mood...

  ... Good or bad as it might be.

Mood (Part One)

We know what moods are, as much as we know what physical pain and pleasure are; indeed, we may be even more intimate with them since our moods accompany us at every moment of our day and lives. Despite this we may tend to ignore, neglect or hide them, as if they were only a disagreeable and dispensable accessory, which we are even ashamed to show to others when it is negative, because it appears to us as a sign of weakness, of fragility, when in fact it is something completely normal for everyone.

To define what mood is, we could say that it is a disposition of the soul, a deep sensation, a mental state that makes us feel better or worse, not physically, but mentally. It's psychological pain or pleasure associated with physical pain or pleasure: two distinct functions that affect each other.

As we did before, we could represent this function on a graph, linking it to descriptive terms that represent our moods' levels: well-being, sadness, delight, and so on.

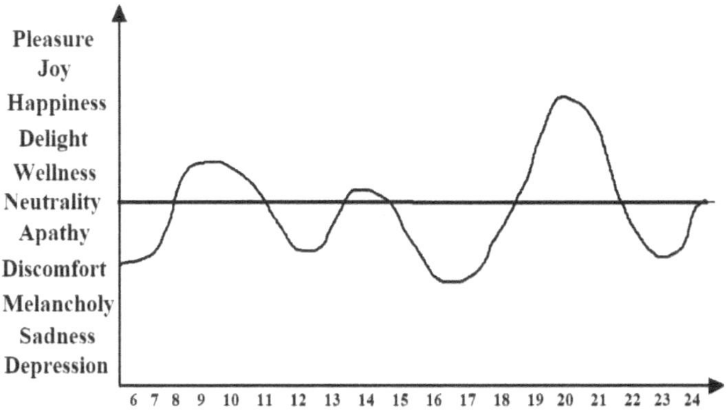

Mood is one of our bodies' many functions; thus, it has to be integral to our survival. Like every other function, it was created by chance and then selected by evolution.

On the other hand, Nature isn't really intelligent and cannot predict if something is going to be useful or harmful; it just creates random functions and then the mechanism of selection establishes order, selecting good and favourable associations between function and environment.

In order to better clarify the concept of biological function, we can compare it to a smartphone application: software that is installed and updated with the aim of improving potential use. A biological function works in the same way: it's an already installed and unchangeable neural program that gives our bodies or our minds additional benefits. This program can't be updated inside a single human being,

30

but it changes with succeeding generations, thanks to genetic mutations and natural selection.

Nature created the psychological pain-pleasure function: joy and happiness, but unfortunately sadness and depression too. If this function exists, though, it means it's good for something, it's useful and it has a specific role; otherwise, its existence would make no sense.

Psychological pain isn't a minor inconvenience or something that can be avoided, but something absolutely necessary for humanity's survival. It's a function created and selected for us, with a defined and determined purpose.

While it's easy to understand the usefulness of the physical pain-pleasure function (that is, defending our physical integrity), the same cannot be said about the psychological pain-pleasure function. What does it protect? Our psychic integrity? Come on, that can't be true.

What is the purpose of the mood function, then? What's the point of psychic pain or pleasure? Why are we sometimes happy and joyful and other times sad and depressed? What advantages could it have? Couldn't we live without mood? Without discomfort, melancholy, sadness; but also, without happiness, gladness, joy…?

What would life be like? Would we act like First Officer Spock? Perhaps we could be happy and joyful twenty-four hours a day and seven days a week? Man, how wonderful that would be!

Evidently, we couldn't always be happy and content; it just didn't suit Nature. But it did suit us, damn it, but in this way, we would surely have become extinct!

There must be a reason behind the existence of this function, because in nature nothing happens by chance and structure, work and energy are never wasted (apart from a peacock's tail). The mood function has to be useful and exist for a reason!

Are you sure? Surely, our moods aren't inevitable; maybe they have no real usefulness or intrinsic value. When something doesn't work in our body, or outside of it, we suffer; this is normal, even obvious. Experience itself has taught us all this. It is unthinkable that we need a specific function to make it happen.

But, it actually isn't so, as pain doesn't exist by and in itself: our body invented and created both the physical and psychological pain thanks to a specific function dedicated to them.

There could be human beings in existence that never suffer, neither physically nor psychologically, but they would soon face extinction, as every form of pain is necessary to make us develop and survive.

Obviously, it should happen in the right measure and never excessively in either direction: we can't feel too much pain or too much pleasure; otherwise, we would fall into the pathological section of the mood function, that is, into depression. This is never to our advantage and exists just because Nature experiments without thinking, roll the dice.

In the case of depressive syndromes, we should be able to update our 'mood' app. Sadly, this is not possible and our only way out is to resort to adequate medical and psychological therapies.

To understand the usefulness of the mood function, we must think about the human species, its survival in its surrounding environment and above all, what allowed it to survive: its strength, size or speed? I don't think these were the qualities!

So, why haven't we faced extinction yet? What mysterious and hidden advantage did we have?

Well, we are just reinventing the wheel… There's not much to the question, because it's clear that our main advantage is and was what's inside our skulls and thus our intellectual and cognitive abilities, relatively greater than those of other animal species (except when we are in love, of course!)

Intelligence alone is not enough. What's moving and guiding this intelligence? Why do we engage in activity? Why are we oriented toward specific goals, those apparently advantageous, and not toward less advantageous ones?

Why do we paint pictures, write poems, create

bridges, design buildings or cars or planes, create companies, find cures for illnesses, discover new lands and send rockets into space? Yes, we need intelligence, but intelligence alone is not enough.

If we are so intelligent, then why are people always so busy, ready to make life more complicated, creating needs and causing problems. Why do we go to such extraordinary lengths?

Why don't we just stop caring about everything and everyone and lounge in the sun from morning to night eating berries and drinking water from a stream?

Now that's what I would call intelligent behaviour! Wouldn't we all be so much better off if we could live like that?

Apparently not. If we had been so well off just doing nothing, we would still be doing it; but that didn't happen because the people who were well off doing nothing are now extinct, and for better or worse, we are still around, in order to feel well, we necessarily have to keep taking action.

The point is that our behaviour patterns need to be advantageous to our survival and the continuation of the human species, but those behaviour patterns need to be guided, encouraged and given value. Lazing around from morning to night isn't to our advantage and so it isn't rewarded, although some people believe the opposite and do everything they can to pursue unproductive behaviour patterns (like spending the whole day at the beach, under an umbrella, doing nothing, trying not to work, taking the elevator instead of the stairs, driving instead of walking, etc).

Now, let's think about ourselves: we always try to do what we like best, that is, something that makes us feel good and increases our emotional well-being, while avoiding things we don't like, that is, those things that have no positive effect on our mood. Let's think about these two mood states: pleasure and feeling good. In the end, they are one and the same: if we like doing something, it means that it makes us feel good.

What does it mean to feel good or bad, anyway? Is it physical pain or pleasure? Absolutely not! To feel good or bad is nothing but psychological pain or pleasure, and therefore relates to the mood function.

If I like a girl, it means that her existence makes me feel good and, when I'm with her, my emotional well-being increases (love). If I don't like a girl, her presence doesn't influence my mood and, so, I don't seek her out (no love).

All of this can only lead to a simple statement: if I do what I like, that is, what makes me feel good, it means that my mood function is guiding my actions and behaviour. It tells me which direction to take and directs me toward one girl rather than another. Who knows what complex algorithm this complicated choice is based on!

Given the results, the algorithm would probably look something like A+B=C.

Basically, Nature's plan for us to avoid intrinsic suffering is to engage in useful activity. Our aim is not action itself, as we often think or believe, but just the positive effect it has on our mood. We do something because it makes us feel good. There isn't any other reason at play: this is our only aim and the real usefulness of the action itself is irrelevant. It is relevant, and useful, only to Nature.

We look for a partner because it makes us feel good-slash-happy, not because we are really interested in him or her.

Mood not only guides our actions but is also the stimulus that forces us to perform those actions whose main aim is to avoid what is after all our normal state of physiological or psychological suffering.

Indeed, while 'at physical and mental rest', humans always tend to a state of suffering (we have been programmed in this way) and the more acute the form suffering, the harder we have to work in order to feel better; if while 'at rest' we were relaxed and at ease, we would have no need to act, and for this reason we would not need to do anything useful.

"If you do nothing, you feel bad, if you act, you feel good."

Now let's try a simple practical example that can help clarify how mood can guide and stimulate our behaviors more clearly: You're alone in a square of your town, walking home for dinner (dinner = food = increase in mood). Suddenly, you notice two good friends in the distance (friends = socialization = increase in mood). At that point, you have a choice to make: to keep walking home to dinner or to call your friends and ask them to have a drink together (drink = alcohol = increase in mood). What choice do you make? Actually, you don't make the choice, because your mood function does it without your knowing.

Both choices increase your emotional well-being, that's true, but one of them would do it more and make you feel really great: that's the second choice. Your aim, however, is not to spend time with your friends but just to feel good.

We are alive just because of what's inside us; everything that is outside our bodies and skins is virtual, illusory and might not even exist. It's just an instrument we use to reach our only true purpose, that is to feel good and heighten our mood, but it also fully reflects the aim of Nature, which is, for us to survive and breed.

§ Dude! What are you talking about? Are you crazy? Just stop for a moment. I don't feel well and my head is spinning. Can I sit down?

According to you, we engage in activity just to feel good? That's it? I wake up in the morning and that's the only purpose of my day? The only purpose of my life?

Yes, that's right. Everything else is just a consequence, but also what we really see and experience every day. In the end it doesn't change much for us, so take it easy!

§ Okay, but if I may say… I'll just sit here a little longer.

If it's true that we act with the only purpose of feeling good, then what improves our mood function? What are the behaviour patterns and actions that make us feel good? What makes us happy and satisfies us, and is useful and productive to us and humankind?

Good, I see you are learning. That's right, you're asking more appropriate questions.

The answer is simple: they are all those actions and behaviour patterns that, unbeknownst to us, for better or for worse, we put into practice every day, or rather we should put into practice every day to feel good: Socializing, thinking, planning, creating, working, helping, discovering, coming up with ideas, loving, acting, fantasizing, playing, searching, learning, sharing, inventing, solving, exploring, etc.

(not money, not fame, not success)

They are all absolutely advantageous behaviour patterns for us and the human species and, conveniently, make us feel good, gratify us and increase our mood. Write them down on a piece of paper and keep the list in your pocket; it may prove to be useful... if you want feel good.

Even drinking, eating and having sex are advantageous and rewarded by making us feel good. And what a feeling! I didn't put them on my list because they are common to all animal species and they are the basis of survival, but the mechanism is the same. In the end, all of them change our mood; in a good way, of course.

Just to give an example of positive behaviour, let's think about creativity: it's one of many things that makes us feel good, being both satisfying and gratifying, and at the same time, it's hugely advantageous to the human species. If humans weren't creative, they would either still be living in caves or be extinct.

Not to mention friendship and the need to socialise: not only do they make us feel good, they have favoured the survival of humankind, because there is strength in unity.

§ What about love?

Well, it's on my list, of course, and I would also add that it's ranked pretty high, the first place actually because it is the most important behavior for the human species, but we will come back to that later.

Unknowingly, every one of us possesses an internal

guide that, like a compass, somehow gives us strength and points in the right direction, driving our behaviour that, obviously, must be sane, positive and sustainable.

In the past, this compass was easier to read and use, because our lives and the world were simpler, more natural and, above all, less fast and chaotic. Nowadays everything is different, more complex and faster, and our internal compasses haven't had the chance to evolve and adjust to those changes. The result is that the 'road signs' today aren't as clear and simple as they were in the past and sometimes we take the wrong road, make wrong turnings and lose ourselves without knowing why. To lose ourselves means needlessly to feel bad.

Basically, we have an old instrument that hasn't had time to adapt…

… But that's what we have, and we're stuck with it!

Mood (Part Two)

Our compass is the instrument that regulates our moods, that drives us and stimulates our actions, our choices and our behaviour. Mood is always present in us and we can't switch it off; in fact, it accompanies us at every moment of our day and life.

It can be positive, neutral or, alas, negative. It can change during the day, from hour to hour or even from minute to minute.

If we represent it on a graph, we can see a curve that continuously goes up and down over time, thus taking a sinusoidal-shaped trend.

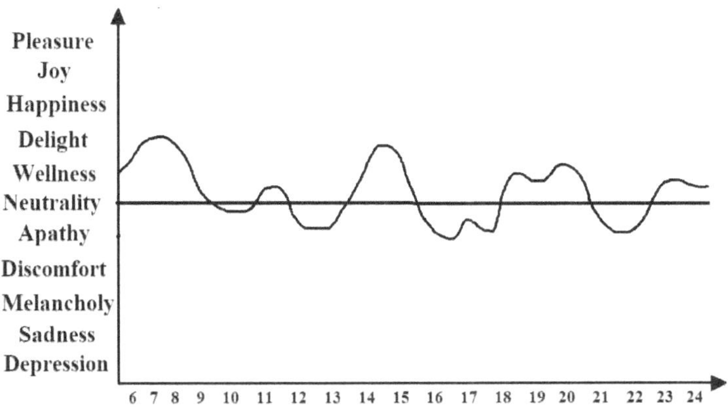

This graph could represent the trend of our moods during a hypothetical day that is devoid of any particular excitement: our moods change from delight

41

to apathy and vice versa, thus it's a relatively quiet day. There might be better or worse days, or days when the good mood or the bad one wins.

The intensity of each spike, either the positive and the negative one, will be variable too, changing from period to period, from situation to situation, and, above all, from person to person since we are not all the same.

I'm not an expert (in the book, I consider the software, how the program works, rather than the hardware, what makes it work and how) but I'm sure I'm not too far off the mark when I say that our moods can be regulated by complex neural or biochemical processes that follow the pharmacodynamic and pharmacokinetic rules applied to several molecules, and that they can depend on several factors that we could subdivide as inside or outside the body and among these also a person's health, the balance between the involved molecules, the physical pain-pleasure function, environment and what happens in it. Above all else, there is the most important factor of all remains our behavior alone, and it is this that truly makes the difference.

The sum of all those factors, both the internal or external and the positive and the negative ones, will decide our mood and how we feel at a specific moment.

These biological laws imply that moods can't

always be positive, that is, above the middle line of our graph – if only they could – even if all external factors of our lives are positive. At the same time, however, they can't always be negative either, that is under the middle line of our graph, even if the whole world is crashing down around us.

All of us dream to always feel good, happy and pleased, but it's just a dream because it's biologically impossible. Both happiness and unhappiness can only be temporary and cyclical, and that's what Nature intended (not without reason), in fact, if we had always felt well, we could not have evolved in this way, and perhaps we would now be extinct.

I would like to give you a small example that will demonstrate how our moods aren't only influenced by external factors, as you might think (the cause of our suffering is external to us, what do I have to do with it?), but also and especially by internal factors.

At first glance, I would say that one of the saddest topics for discussion out there is death, especially our own. This topic should always depress us, but that's not always true:

1) We think about death and it makes us sad: the decrease in our mood is due to a negative external factor, 'death'.

2) We are sad and we think about death: we are already sad and that's why we think about

death. Sadness is not caused by the thought of death; sadness is already there, maybe without a reason, and it makes us think about death, as if to justify the discomfort we feel.

3) Sometimes we are happy and peacefully talk about death, and it doesn't change our good mood at all.

In the above cases, the negative external factor is always there, yet mood and situations are really different.

Even the bad experiences from our past can make us feel bad, painful memories, grief, losses, but sometimes they are not the real cause of our suffering as we believe. Sometimes, when we feel bad without a specific reason (suffering is physiological), painful memories resurface in our mind, almost as if to justify the pain we are feeling at that moment. And this is how a bad memory can mistakenly become, for us, the eternal cause of our suffering.

Love and The Compass

How does love influence our moods? How does our compass behave next to a pretty girl?

Without any doubt the compass needle would go completely crazy and insistently point toward the poor unfortunate woman and no other factor would be able to change its direction.

The reason why our relationship influences our compass and our moods so intensely and so positively is obvious: relationships are essential for humanity's survival; since they're so important – indeed, supremely so – they must be generously rewarded!

§ What are you talking about? A reward? Money? Holidays? A car?

Come on! The only reward at Nature's disposal: a spike in our mood, topped in this case by physical pleasure, which never hurts.

Do you remember the first chapter?

Love substantially increases our moods in general, and our sinusoid is solidly projected on the upper side of our graph. What could be better than that? And the beauty of it all is that it will exist forever, for the rest of your life, till death do us part, at least as far as the official documents poems, movies, songs are concerned.

If only it were true! Alas, we already know that it's not possible: nothing lasts forever in our biological model. In fact, this idea doesn't correspond to the reality that, sooner or later, every couple will have to face.

Instead of 'forever', I'd prefer to say: 'for a fair period of time'; at least until the sad and inexorable decline toward the lower side of our graph. From then on, it gets ugly!

Of course, during that 'fair period of time' we feel good, damn it, and that's why the temptation to fall for it again is so strong in all of us. You can see the consequences just looking around you!

To reiterate the undisputed strength of love compared to any other behavior , let's think back to the previous example, being in 'that' square and the choices made by our 'mood' app. If you don't remember it, it was about choosing between walking home for dinner or going out with friends; they were both positive choices, but one of them was more positive (double positive factor, socialization + alcohol).

After making your instinctive choice, you're walking with your dearest friends toward the bar, happy and upbeat. Suddenly the stunning, irresistible female friend you're secretly in love with appears on the horizon. You would rather die than be there, and if you could, you'd gladly dig a hole then and there for your friends because they are preventing you from making a third choice, which would also also be the best for your emotional well-being since it would skyrocket you into outer space to invite her out!

(love is the strongest behavior of all)

Alas, you look around and can't find any hole where to bury your friends; you're also a good man and would never do anything like that. Like a beaten dog, you drag yourself toward the bar mournfully and greet your beautiful female friend with a faint voice.

Don't worry: you can be sure that your mood will increase to where it was before the third choice presented itself, that is, before you knew there was even a third choice…

… Especially after a spritz.

<u>The three choices:</u>

1) Home   →   Good (Well-being)

2) Friends   →   Better (Happiness)

3) Female friend →   Best (Pleasure)

Did you choose? No, your 'mood' app did it.

-Instinct is the thing that makes you feel best-

The Macaque

'Falling head-over-heels-in-love with a woman' might be a cliché, but we have all experienced it, for better or for worse. Who can deny it? Indeed, when we fall in love we fall head-over-heels, and that's an obvious and undeniable truth: our psyche is altered, our behaviour changes and the world around us appears different to us.

A similar effect, however, can be achieved even if you are not in love; in fact, the mere presence of a woman next to a man is enough to alter something in his head. It's irrelevant whether he knows her or not in to order to achieve this effect; on the contrary, free fantasy is better. As long as a 'characteristic' physical aspects adds to the explosive fantasy of the man, he's done for, with absolutely predictable and repeatable results.

(what simple and foolish beings we are)

It is said that even science has studied this phenomenon and it appears that it's due to the functional inhibition of some specific cognitive areas of the brain that, collectively, have been defined as a 'Suppressed Area' (probably to emphasise that, under those conditions, a man behaves like an idiot).

They have also demonstrated that next to this 'Suppressed Area' another area of the brain exists, consisting of extremely simple and archaic cortical structures, and it has been defined as an 'On-Off Area'. This area, whose function is still uncertain, generates extremely simple and stereotypical ancestral responses when its owner receives specific sound and visual stimulation; in the end, those responses take the form of a series of lower and less noble behaviour patterns, that I can only describe as trivial and vulgar.

No, no, Prince Charming doesn't behave like that… Don't worry, ladies: he doesn't have an On-Off Area, let alone trivial and vulgar behaviour. That's impossible!

Next to a beautiful woman, a man's cognitive abilities are comparable to those of an adult *Macaca sylvanus* or Barbary macaque, something that must have inspired Italy's legendary Paolo Conte while writing his songs.

Their impact on a man is still mysterious and unexplained; in fact, their role and importance in the evolution of the human race are still unknown.

As a fun exercise, when you see a man on the street next to an attractive woman, try to think of the macaque inside him that is manifesting at that moment, and observe carefully his instinctive and basic behavior: truly amusing.

Why does the mere presence of a woman cause the reduction of a man's cognitive abilities and his perception of reality? Why did evolution select this mechanism of mental obfuscation that inevitably induces a state of severe weakness and vulnerability to external events in men? What's the point in weakening him so much? Why make him into a fool?

Is it not better for a man to be strong and healthy, with an intact and functioning ability to reason?

Evidently, a man with his rational faculty intact is disadvantageous to the survival of the human race at this point.

This odd and curious mechanism is completely reversible in a healthy man: in fact, if the triggering factor – the woman – is taken away, his mental faculties come back again at full capacity and in a very short time. The same mechanism is irreversible and lasts through time, however, when a man is struck by the 'falling-in-love disease'.

Why is all of this happening? Have you ever thought about it? Have any idea? I suppose you don't, and even scientists haven't been able to give any definite answers.

Despite this, I'd like to suggest a possible answer. Let's say that I've had a small insight. For goodness' sake, it might be nonsense or totally absurd, and it's probably wrong, but…

Maybe… It might be… What if a man endowed with reason and with intact cognitive faculties could never date a woman? What if a lucid, thinking man with the power of discernment could never mate with anyone? This would lead to the extinction of our species, though. Farewell, mankind.

No, please, it can't be true. That's impossible!

But if that truly was the case, since this is the result of evolution, in the past there might have been men without this evolutionary feature. They were endowed with reason and would keep their distance from any woman they saw. Forget flattery and courtship (not to mention presents!)

Of course, all of this means that they said goodbye to procreation and to the continuation of their lineage; because of this characteristic, they became extinct, poor things! In essence, evolution chose this mechanism that makes men dumb just to allow mating between them and women. Well, if someone ever manages to demonstrate my theory, it would be interesting, at the very least!

§ Sorry, but if no man endowed with reason could ever be with a woman, then that would imply that being with a woman is a mistake and no one realises it.

Yes, that's right: being with a woman is a serious mistake, but it's the only mistake that allows the human race to survive. Consequently, it isn't a real mistake but a state of necessity.

'Is that actually true, though? Maybe I've got slightly carried away. Did I get caught up in the excitement? No, please, it can't be true; if it were, it would mean that we are constantly deceived, tricked and rendered ridiculous. Surely that is impossible? We are not stupid!'

Ah, nature … It's eternally surprising and magnificent.

Switching Couples

There was a time when I too was struck by the illness of falling-in-love. In my case, however, for some reason, a part of my Suppressed Area was still alive and kicking, as well as my On-Off Area, of course. That goes without saying, I'm hardly Prince Charming, after all.

This area of my brain, that was uninvolved and anaesthetised by the 'magnificent' love process, continuously posed questions and proffered doubts and perplexities about the concept of the relationship that should have been linear, unambiguous and long-lasting, but that wasn't so linear, unambiguous and especially long-lasting, after all.

One Saturday evening, I had the unfortunate urge to voice my doubts and legitimate perplexities to my beloved of the moment. I wish I hadn't done so! Here is a description of that disastrous evening.

It was a beautiful, hot summer's day, and I had just driven almost fifty miles to see her. I had spent the day thinking and dreaming her and I was full of joy and anticipation. I couldn't wait to see, hug and be near her.

When I arrived at my destination, I saw her, beautiful and fascinating as always; we were finally together. Happily, we headed down to a pub to have a drink (I prefer cafés, but there weren't any).

We were sitting at a small table, under the influence of soft lighting and suffused candlelight, love and alcohol. Around us were other couples of young lovers sitting at small tables like ours.

Looking around a bit, and feeling happy and relaxed, I observed the others, confident that nothing could ever spoil that wonderful evening.

Alas, that cursed small area of my brain, not anaesthetised by love or my powerful B-52 cocktail, came into full swing and started to think, reflect and reason about the familiar situation at the pub with all those happy couples in love like us. At first, the inner voice was innocuous enough, but then, since the area is unfortunately linked to my vocal chords, it all turned into an inevitably and catastrophically foul soliloquy.

Thus, I said: 'Think about it, my dear: there's no doubt that we are made for each other, and that we'll always be together, swimming in a sea of love. There are billions of men and billions of women in the world, but we met anyway, almost by chance; just think how lucky we are. I'm so happy and excited when I'm near you. I love you, adore you and always think about you. I want you every day…'

While saying that, I held her hand. Oh, what a sentimentalist I am!

Let's make an estimate: 2.5 billion women and 2.5 billion men. What's the probability of meeting you? I don't really remember statistics, but I guess that it is 2.5 billion to one. Boy, it's like winning the lottery! It confirms that I was really lucky when I meet you.

Moving ahead, however, we must think that as we speak the other men surrounding us have the same probability to meet their better half. If we consider all of those probabilities, it comes out as a big number, a really huge number. Tonight, in this pub, a miracle of destiny has just happened.

What if we sum up the probabilities of all the pubs in this province? In Italy? In the whole world?

Ahhhh! I'm beginning to feel desperate!

We get a huge, unthinkable number that approaches infinity; thus, the probability is practically absolute zero.

What do I mean by absolute zero? The probability that you are my better half is absolute zero? But... But... But... But does that mean that romantic love is basically impossible? That it doesn't exist? Something doesn't quite add up!

No, my reasoning is correct. It's clear that maths and statistics strongly oppose the idea that you're the right person for me: for all intents and purposes, the idea is impossible.

Ahhhh! Yet more desperate!

Thinking about it and considering Planck's constant and the theory of special relativity, there are only two sustainable possibilities. The first one is that there are a multitude of people right for me, in which this case, so long to all my poems and my dreams, because it would mean that being with you or being with someone else would be the same. The second possibility has the same tragic conclusion as the first one: the right person doesn't exist, thus being with you or being with someone else would be the same!

Ahhhh! My desperation overwhelms me!

Damn it, this is a serious problem to solve. We can't just let the myth of love be destroyed by two simple, small Year 10 maths formulas!

I didn't talk about maths and statistics to my partner, but I tried to give her a simple practical example to demonstrate the lack of sustainability of the Prince Charming fairy tale.

Thus, I said: 'Think about it, love: I'm telling you beautiful things about us, but I'm sure that the other couples sitting at the tables around us are repeating the same, identical words. Look at them: they are in love like us and are having the same thoughts, desires, feelings of happiness. They are saying the same things and are holding hands just like us.

'We are very lucky, aren't we? But they are too. Everybody is lucky tonight at this café. Sorry, love, I meant at this pub.

'Think again about it: our first meeting was definitely random, absolutely not programmed or planned, but theirs was too. We could say that destiny brought us together and not our own will (I was about to enter a minefield). For this very reason and more, and from a purely theoretical point of view, trying to be pragmatic, I believe that if, by a bizarre twist of fate, magic or any other reason, we were to switch partners at random, I'm sure that we would hear the same words and phrases I've just uttered to you. If we switched a second time, at random again, of course, nothing would change: same phrases, same thoughts, same emotions, same convictions, and even the same beliefs.

'If all of this is true, my love, then something isn't working and is eluding us. Sometimes I feel confused, perplexed… What about you, my love? What do you think?'

Ahhhh! Help, this is a tragedy!

My partner's eyes have turned from sweet and understanding to dark, corrosive and menacing in the blink of an eye. I could see thunder, wind, lightning, hail and an entire storm behind her offended gaze. Our night was ruined!

With my tail between my legs, I quickly drove back my fifty miles and returned home, or rather, and thankfully, I returned to my friends at the café. Forget that damn pub!

Ah, I was misunderstood! From that day on, I realised that some ideas are best kept to oneself for everyone's comfort…

… At least for now.

Falling in Love

§ Love! My soul! How much love I feel for you! Finally, I have found true love, love that is eternal and infinite. I'm linked to you only by love, thus by definition: generosity, altruism, a wish for your happiness and well-being; all of this without asking for anything in return, of course…

… And finally, I feel happiness and the joy of being alive.

What? Finally? Happiness? Joy? Please repeat what you just said. So, you are happy now? Do you feel at peace with yourself and the world around you?

Do you remember my talk about evolution, mood, rewards and the famous compass? What do you think about your fundamental behaviour toward your partner? Is it advantageous for the human race and thus does it deserve a reward? You said: 'Finally I feel happiness,' not me. Just think a little about your mood sinusoid and where it's going right now!

§ Yes, that is true. Indeed, thinking about it, I can't deny that my life has improved significantly thanks to my partner, and my sinusoid has moved a bit higher in my mood graph.

In fact, I have received something in return, but I'm not with her for this reason. Of course, when you receive love, you also receive well-being and happiness, but you don't love someone just for the sake of feeling good! You love only because of the love you have in your heart and in the depths of your soul, and that you want to give and share with the other person.

Love, my soul, you don't believe in that nonsense about evolution and advantages and rewards as put forward by this imbecile, do you? Only my eternal and infinite love binds me to you, not the fact that it makes me feel good and fills me with joy and happiness. I'm definitely not selfish!

Sorry, I'm going to ask you a fundamental question: if your relationship with your partner didn't make you feel good, increase your mood and give you so much joy and peacefulness, would you still be with her? Would you still look forward to being with her? Would you work so hard at it?

§ If it didn't make me feel good, you say? Well, I mean… Bah… Indeed… Hypothetically speaking, do you mean if I didn't feel good with her? If I wasn't happy with her and felt nothing?

That's right.

§ But… Maybe yes… Maybe no… I guess… Well… Let me think about it… If this person doesn't make me feel good and being with them isn't joyful, then it's not love, that's easy; thus, it would make no sense to be together! Did I answer right? Come on, I handled that well, didn't I!

So, are you saying – let me get this straight – that if this person doesn't make you feel good and give you joy and happiness, then that's not true love?

§ Mmmh, yes, it should be like that… If you don't feel good with a person and aren't happy with them… Obliviously it's not love. Even a child would understand that!

Aaah! You said it! Good! Congratulations, you're reasoning! Can I chisel your fantastic and spot-on answer on marble? With a simple answer, you explained everything. And you did this all by yourself.

You might not understand your answer yet, but I can assure you that it's not only right but crystal clear. You're fantastic, a true friend and a true collaborator.

Ah, this is life… This is love… This is what being in love is…

Getting to Know Each Other

Let's talk again about the statistical improbability of finding your better half. Do you remember it? 2.5 billion men, the same number of women, the unsustainable Prince Charming fairy tale and everything else?

The thing is, finding your better half is not only a mathematical impossibility, but also a perfect waste of time. We believe ourselves to be intelligent and sophisticated, but in reality, we are much simpler and dumber than we think we are. I don't mean On-Off, but almost. Often our behaviour follows extremely simple, trivial and predictable rules and everything else is 'whipped cream' created on purpose by our skilled creativity and imagination.

But it is this "whipped cream" that then confuses us and makes us lose the thread, because it unnecessarily complicates simple things.

We think and believe that we have to find our perfect love, but we don't. We don't need to find our better half to make a relationship work; this is a condition that Nature has established as neither necessary nor imperative. That's because every little human being always and in any case falls in love with a person that they don't fundamentally know and don't even need to know.

We may only have a vague idea of who our partner truly is, but this condition of unawareness is irrelevant as far as our relationship is concerned, because the game created by Nature doesn't work that way.

If you want to get to know a person, the first thing you need is their sincerity (and you rarely get it), then you need time, a lot of it, that translates into years and years of honest and close coexistence.

We already struggle to know ourselves, even after a lifetime, let alone another person that, among other things, is so 'biologically' different from us!

§ Wait, how do we fall in love with someone we don't really know? What the heck have we fallen in love with?

We never fall in love with a real and specific person – let's call them X – we think we know; we fall in love with the idea of them, an idea that we know very well and could call Y. This idea is part of us and a stereotype that we unknowingly apply to that person as if it were a sticker.

Do you remember the lovers in the pub that we could swap at random? Nothing would have changed for them, and their words of love would have been the same. The people of each couple, X, would have changed, but the ideas they had about the other, Y, would not have, because they are an incontestable constant.

We don't have enough time to truly get to know each other because that's a luxury nature cannot afford: if mating happened only after we truly got to know each other, then the human race would have already become extinct a long time ago. Therefore, since we can barely know each other, it doesn't matter if we date a person or another, because we live on Y constants and not X variables.

The Y idea within us is artificial and subconscious and has nothing to do with reality; it's pure fantasy and a dream and this is how we want it.

We are the greatest and most talented dreamers, just as good at disregarding reality as never changing our ideas in order not to ruin everything!

In the case of lovers, there's no deafness worse than that of a person who doesn't want to hear, even with all the evidence staring them in the face. Thus, we live on dreams and illusions, with the selfish aim of feeling good and being happy. Obviously, it can't last forever, because no one can live on Y; sooner or later, you have to realise that the real and complex X does exist...

... And if your X is the wrong one, it's your problem!

Chicken Leg Theory

Falling in love with a girl is like having a delicious, tasty, well roasted and steaming chicken leg at your disposal. You eat, taste and bite it here and there and you feel happy.

Hmmm, all that goodness, that pleasure, that well-being, that joy! Life smiles at you, or rather your belly smiles at you. I mean, you're in good spirits, happy and satisfied as you are with your culinary trophy. What else could you ever want from life?

You keep eating, though, and the meat is gone. Inevitably, you find the hard bone at some point. *Tung*! You're surprised and ask yourself: 'But how has this happened? What am I going to do now?'

Then, you turn the leg around without worrying too much, find more meat and resume eating. Ahh! Contentment!

Then the unhappy event strikes again. *Tung*! Luckily, there's still meat: you turn the leg around and keep eating without thinking about it.

The meat on that leg, however, is not infinite and it will be gone completely at some point, leaving only a hard and unpalatable bone. You stop, because you can't pretend that nothing is happening, like you did before – you're a master of that – and with your eyes wide open you ask yourself: 'What should I do now? Who can help me?'

At this point in life, you reach a tragic and inexorable crossroads that makes you choose between biting the bone and nibbling on it for the rest of life, like a dog (it's not that bad, after all), or trading it for another chicken leg.

If you trade it for another leg, you resume eating meat; thus, you get enjoyment, gratification and well-being again. History, however, doesn't change but repeats itself and after a while you find yourself back at the crossroads.

What should you do, then? Should you keep trading every bone for another chicken leg, or settle down and nibble on the bone for the rest of your life?

Someone could suggest an intermediate position: a bone to nibble on at home and a secret chicken leg on the outside, a reserve of well-being and excitement. All of this, however, could only work if the choice were 'bipartisan'; alas, the time is not ripe right now and this could become a very dangerous game because it implies the real risk of destroying your family and the not-negligible consequence of finding yourself with two women being in charge of your life!

'Why deliberately choose two crosses when one is enough?'

What do you think, my dear friend? What can you tell us about your marriage? How long did it last? Almost six years, if I'm not mistaken…

§ Boy, here we go again … Weren't we supposed to not see each other again? Yeah, six years, as you just said. It's very simple so I'll make a long story short.

Of those six long years, the first two were nice, the third one so-so and from the fourth one onward something changed. She changed. Our relationship was wrecked and worn out and with time our enthusiasm and our desire to be together plummeted. In the end, the passion was gone and we were getting on each other's nerves.

We had become friends, or like brother and sister. We still loved each other, that's true, but she evidently was the wrong person and I had realised it too late.

Now that we aren't together any more, I hope to start all over again and to finally find the right person, real love this time, as I have always dreamed of doing.

Yes, I more or less remember it. I'm really sorry because you truly loved each other.

So, you're sure she was the wrong person for you, are you? Had there been someone else in her place, things would have gone very differently? Am I right?

§ Of course, things would have gone very differently: if she had been the right person, then our relationship wouldn't have ended and we would still love each other. I don't understand what you mean.

I hate to disappoint you, but it doesn't work that way. The reality is that it would have been the same with any other person, for better or for worse. Or rather, it wouldn't have been exactly the same but it would have ended the same way. Couples drift apart because they aren't happy any more, there's no passion and complicity, their emotions become flat, and they have the erroneous belief that they have married the wrong person. It happens to every couple, even to the ones that don't give up and stay together. Unfortunately, the meat on the bone comes to an end for everyone.

The meat represents the dream, the illusion, the myth of undying love, the fairy tale, the sticker you glued on your partner. The bone is reality: what you truly are without fantasies and illusions.

As we all know, the first bestows strong emotions and our emotions cannot help but skyrocket in our graph, and this makes us feel happy and satisfied. Reality as a bone doesn't have those fantastic and beneficial effects on our emotions; let's say it just has an acceptable and neutral survival effect.

The first phase of a relationship is just a fantasy cleverly controlled by our will, while the second phase is precisely reality and, alas, there's nothing we can do about it. We can't shape it as we please: it is what it is, with the strengths and weaknesses of each of us!

People never change; thus, we have to accept them the way they are and for what they are, focusing on their strengths and trying not to linger too much on their weaknesses. Alas, usually couples do exactly the opposite.

You don't think you can change someone, do you? Wasted breath: it's an impossible task and you'll come out defeated, disappointed and with broken bones. This is not the right direction to take.

We already said that when we meet someone, we don't really know them; we subconsciously just create a concept of whom we want them to be, that is our ideal partner or a stereotypical model, full of good qualities and devoid of flaws.

'But how, love? When we met, you were so different. Over the years, you have changed, somehow.'

She actually was always like that and you just needed to lift the wool from your eyes to understand it. Moreover, don't forget that you can't put new meat on your chicken leg, that is, revitalise your relationship. It's impossible and it would be a waste of time: an exercise in therapeutic obstinacy.

If you think about it, however … There is something that could completely revitalise a relationship with a partner and bring back the meat on the leg: a concussion that causes retrograde amnesia. After the total cancellation of one's memory, you can start over with your romantic love, passionate and dreamy. Obviously, as we all know, it would work only for a limited period of time!

Senile dementia could help us, too. Every morning I could wake up and, rolling over in bed, I could ask: 'Who is this?'

In this case, love could truly be eternal…

… But we won't be us!

Marriage

We have finally made it to the insidious fork in the road, the choice we must make, Hamlet's dilemma; we choose rightly, in a mature and steady fashion, the road that leads to stable family life. In short, let's face it: in the end we choose the bone.

Why don't they tell us the truth?

§ No, no! Are you crazy? They can't!

And here we have the fable of marriage, almost a myth, served on a plate.

Is it true you're getting married? Oh, that's great! You'll be great together, and you'll surely be happy. I'm so happy for you… What a beautiful thing! It will be wonderful, magnificent! A marriage to remember…

Everybody says the same thing: upbeat messages that cannot but make you hope for a bright and peaceful future. Things kick into gear and you jump in feet first with courage and confidence, thinking only beautiful, positive thoughts. Of course, after what they said… Why would they lie? Why does no one show their true cards?

§ No, no! I already told you they can't. Shh! Keep it down or they'll hear you. Shh! Quiet, please. My wife is here! Nice, it's so nice to get married, you know? Marriage!

What are you scared of? Why is no one able to tell the truth about marriage, in a rush of sincerity? The true essence of this institution? But no! Everybody hides and turns a blind eye, saying that everything is fine. Everyone apparently is delighted. Why all these sugar-coated lies?

Anyway, the direct consequence of this myth is that people get married under the best auspices, with high expectations of happiness, love, freedom and the idea of starting a beautiful, peaceful, perfect nuclear family.

Alas, reality hits you in the face eventually, because marriage is synonymous with a narrow, closed co-habitation. Damn! Forget being able to go back to your own pad, like you did when you started dating. That is water under the bridge.

Men and women are deeply different beings in taste, needs, mentality and more, but they are forced, by marriage, to live in close and closed proximity every day. Always together and side by side, inevitably colliding and getting on each other's nerves. Choices then become a difficult compromise that never satisfy anyone in the end... And goodbye freedom!

To complicate matters, as if that wasn't enough, children enter the picture. At that point, you'd normally think: 'Well, now that we have children together surely things will get better and everything will be fine.' Everything gets worse, instead: your relationship with your partner is drastically limited as your children take up all of your time, and they effectively become additional cohabitants of our lives, and you will also have to say goodbye to the little freedom that you may have barely managed to earn. At that point, only the strongest survive, or rather, make marriage survive.

This kind of coexistence surely is against nature, and anything against nature, doesn't do us any good. The further away you get from a natural, simple and primitive life, the more you feel uncomfortable and suffer. You shouldn't make the mistake of thinking that your discomfort is due to the wrong person living with you, as everyone thinks (you may have some doubts after your second wedding, replaced by absolute certainty after your third), but it's due to the narrow limitations imposed by marriage itself.

If you want to verify what I have just said, just take your best friend, who shares the same passions, interests and ideas of a perfect evening as you do, and go and live with him under the same roof, as if you were married. You'll see that friction, fights and misunderstandings will soon ensue as well as the desire for your own place.

Alternatively, you could clone yourself and live with your clone. You'd be perfectly identical, with the same interests, ideas, needs, etc. Even then, there would be friction, fights and misunderstanding like in a real marriage.

By their very nature, humans needs to live with others, but they also needs freedom and privacy. If they don't get all of it, they suffer.

To live well, you need the right balance in all respects; marriage, however, isn't well balanced, as we have already seen. You can try to create your own balance together with communication and sympathy, leaving the right amount of space and freedom. Basically, you need to put a patch on something that had a hole in it in the first place.

It's not easy to define common and personal areas and their boundaries within a couple. Usually, it's the woman who sets the pace: 'You and I, my love, forever one. We'll do and share everything together!'

Haha! Wait a minute. The animal man also needs a personal and untouchable space that is his and only his. If you want to make a relationship work, you must avoid a complete overlap of a man's and a woman's lives; a partial, I would say 80%, overlap is enough. Who's bidding lower? I do!

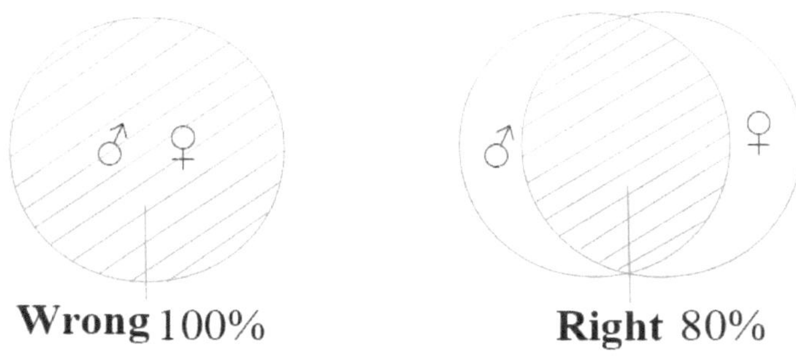

Wrong 100%   **Right** 80%

When children enter the picture, the balance changes to the detriment of both your personal and shared spaces.

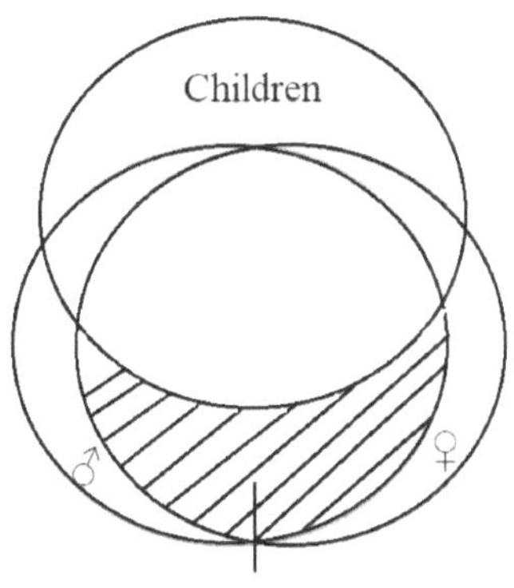

Shared space by a couple 10-20%

Thus, a couple's relationship, and each one's life, can only go from bad to worse, unless the couple understands and accepts the need each has for personal space.

Anyway, to make the marriage work, no one should

ever renounce his or her right to a personal and untouchable space, that should be controlled in full autonomy and used in the best possible way. Take that paper you have in your pocket, the list of things that make you feel good, and feel free to make many of them, varied and…

…Best of luck!

Theorem

Do you know Marco Ferradini's song? Well, the title alone is already a tad unsettling since it should be about love; despite this, the beauty of that song is undeniable. In its initial verses, the song demonstrates that love isn't exactly what bonds a couple…

Take a woman, tell her you love her…

… And rest assured she will leave you.

Take a woman, treat her badly …

… And you'll see she'll love you.[1]

But how can this be? Shouldn't it be the other way around?

Still, those verses are contain some and are yet another confirmation that love isn't the main ingredient in a romantic relationship, nor the dominant one. In fact, even if it were completely absent, the 'sauce' could still be made, and what a sauce!

But why would a 'mistreated' woman bind to her partner more? And why would a well-treated woman tend to get tired and run away? What is the reason for this inconsistency? It seems paradoxical.

[1] Original verses: *Prendi una donna, dille che l'ami […] e sta' sicuro che ti lascerà […] Prendi una donna, trattala male […] e allora sì vedrai che t'amerà.* Pagani, H. and Ferradini, M. (1981). Teorema [Recorded by M. Ferradini]. On *Schiavo senza catene* [Mini-LP]. Italy: Spaghetti Records.

We are playing with the same ingredients again here: the mood function and the factors influencing it.

Let's try to represent these two different situations on our 'mythical' mood graph and see how the different couple's relationships affect its trend: the relationship where the woman is treated like a princess and provided with every consideration, and the relationship where the woman is mistreated in a condescending way and with little or no consideration for her needs.

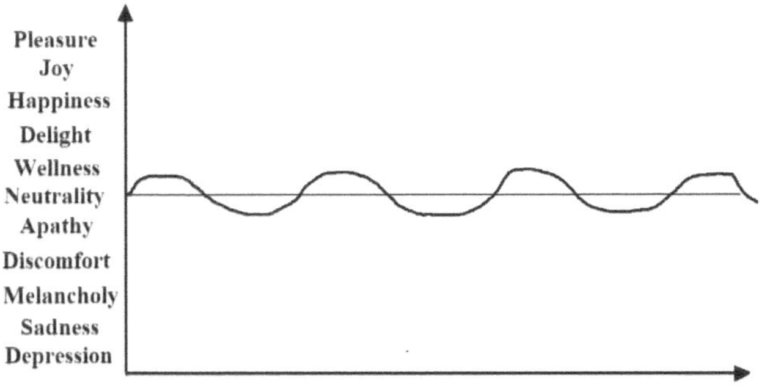

A well-treated woman:

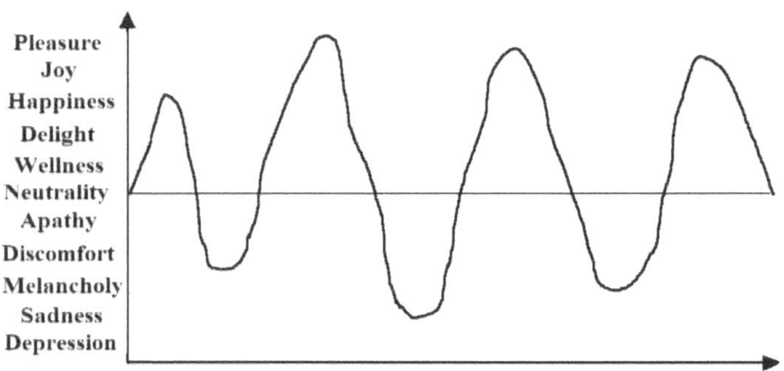

A mistreated woman:

(Of course, it goes without saying that I'm not talking about physical abuse but only psychological and behavioural abuse)

That's why a woman who is wrapped up in cotton wool gets bored, as the songs says: the curve of her mood tends to flatten in relation to the couple's relationship.

A quiet, serene, protected and uneventful love life! Isn't that a good thing? Isn't that what they are looking for from their partners?

In theory yes: that's exactly what everyone wants from their partners. In this way, however, the intense positive mood spikes are missing, and with them also the excitement and passion, which are a direct consequence of the lack of the negative ones.

A purely quiet and peaceful relationship excludes the passion that must be sought elsewhere, but to do that, you have to get busy, look around, search, act and … get cracking on your list!

In a well-treated woman, only positive factors related to the couple's relationship are present, whereas in a poorly treated woman, negative factors are also present. This makes her mood more dynamic, with continuous ups and downs alternating. Sometimes she feels bad, suffering justified, but then, by rebound, she can also feel very good; therefore, strong emotions are always alive, present, and, importantly, remain in memory and become associated with that specific partner (a partner whom the woman will continue to seek for her illusory sense of well-being, even if objectively wrong).

Ironically, all of this can make a couple's relationship more intense and long-lasting, even if more tumultuous.

Of course, after you marry such a 'difficult' partner the damage is done and life is ruined. Women are good…

… At making these kinds of mistakes!

Postulates of Love

Let's try to draw some conclusions now. We can take stock of the situation and define the fundamental rules that regulate a couple's relationship… The real ones, I mean.

Luckily, there aren't that many. There are only three 'postulates' concerning love. You will immediately notice that they clash badly with the commonly accepted concept of love, which, in fact, stands in diametrical opposition to them. The three postulates are: blindness, selfishness and finality.

1) **Blindness**. We fall in love with someone we don't know.
2) **Selfishness**. We fall in love only and exclusively for ourselves.
3) **Finality**. Everything always must come to an end.

Thus, we fall in love with who-knows-who, we do it only to receive gifts (and not for a great and noble reason we should be proud of) and for a limited period of time.

Where's love? A love that permeates our hearts!

Evidently, this isn't about love, because following those three conditions, it is excluded by definition.

What bonds a couple, if not love? What serves as a magnet and glue? What's that thing we feel within us?

A feeling so strong, so intense and apparently so noble and deep that impetuously pushes us toward our partner with relentless force?

Well, I would say that the answer is clear (drum roll): it's that thing that guides our actions, our behaviour and our choices. It's that thing that makes us feel good or bad, it's our pleasure and suffering, it's our joy and pain.

Whatever people describe in their poems, novels, films or songs doesn't really exist. It's all fake, just an 'apparent force', like gravity, but we have always believed in it with blind, untouchable faith, especially because that's what we've been taught.

That's what it is, what guides us and what makes us look around, meet and come together. The driving force is our pleasure, our joy, our will and our need to feel good, it is the constant need to soothe our physiological suffering. Thus, what makes us meet and bond isn't the power of **love**, but the power of the less poetic and noble **mood**! Right, the words are similar but they certainly are not the same thing! (**Amore** ed **Umore**)

Our selfishness guides us and makes us move; it's our compass and our app and it directs us where to go to feel good. It's not love. Love exists, but it's something else.

There goes the myth, the dream and the pleasure to dream: statistics, calculation of probabilities, X and Y variables, functions, applications, graphs, macaques, joy and pain!

But how can we ruin such a beautiful dream so cruelly, I wonder? A dream that is shared, consolidated and ingrained by centuries of human history! It's barbaric! And yet, this is reality. It's not like we can pretend everything's fine, can we?

Well, it could be a good idea. Why spoil all of these good things with reality, after all? We should think about it for a moment.

Oh, love! Rivers of poems, novels, songs…
… Or is it all just mood?

Wrapped up in Cotton Wool

This is what we have in our hearts, or rather, in our minds. This is what binds us to our partner. Forget great, magnificent, eternal love! If only it was that!

Well, in fact, and luckily, there surely is a bit of love in our hearts – I already said that it has a right to exist – but it's difficult to make it emerge or prevail over our more powerful moods and thus, in the end, over our selfishness.

Selfishness brings us together, but then it's the same thing that divides us.

Let's get something straight: we all are selfish, there's no denying or refusing it. We were born this way, so it's not totally our fault. Evidently, our selfishness endows us and our species with many advantages since it's the most common characteristic of mankind.

Actually, it's correct to be a little selfish, and thus to put ourselves first before others, because if we want to help someone else, we must necessarily be strong and in good health first and foremost.

It's a bit like being racist: the truth is that we all are, because it's in our nature and we were programmed this way. It doesn't mean we should act in this way, though: it's a legacy of our past that should be erased using common sense and our innate intelligence.

Rights and obligations should be the same for

everyone, regardless of sex, race or gender.

When we are born, we should all have the same rights and obligations and the same future life opportunities, but, for purely economic reasons, it rarely happens. We should all start from the same point and advance only because of merit; in order to do that, we need a strong social state that is able to give everyone the opportunity to study through to graduation without financial commitment. The advantages of this healthy selection would benefit all of us. Sadly, it doesn't work that way right now.

Very well, let's talk about mood again. We should ask ourselves: if we truly managed to remove all negative external factors in our lives, thus creating a dream existence, wouldn't we really always feel good? Wouldn't we always be happy and content? Or, is it not true that our mood would slump anyway, sooner or later?

The answer to the last question is yes. Unfortunately, this is how the human machine works. Nature chose this and anything else is incompatible.

We engage in activity precisely to avoid this physiological suffering. Without it, we would spend our days idling, eating berries and drinking water from a stream. All of this is verifiable experimentally because there already are living beings that live in this happy condition of life, thus with a total lack of negative external factors!

§ And who are those extremely lucky beings?

My children, when they were in preschool age. They were mollycoddled, protected and the centre of everyone's attention, always ready to play and have fun. They didn't suffer hunger, thirst, cold, heat or solitude. They were living in a world of being permanently mollycoddled, obsessively protected by their parents, grandparents and all other relatives.

Negative external factors? Nowhere in sight, luckily for them. What about their mood? Was it definitely high and long-lasting? Were they always calm and smiling?

If only they were! Unfortunately, we have already seen that it's impossible: in fact, suffering and discomfort exists even for them. Alas, when children suffer, they change, become nervous and hateful and have a tendency to behave badly. All of this makes them clash head-on with their poor parents, followed by scolding, inconsolable sobbing, and a subsequent restorative sleep.

Then, as if by magic, as in the calm after the storm, they feel well and are peaceful again, with a desire to play as if nothing had happened. Why do they follow this cyclical behaviour?

Because our moods are cyclical. Don't forget the graph, the inexorable sinusoid and the factors regulating it.

In that case, the external factors were only positive, that's true, but unfortunately there were also internal factors at play the intrinsic mechanism of mood . The latter caused the gradual mood, slumps and thus the onset of suffering that was seemingly unmotivated.

All of this demonstrates that, in the end, being mollycoddled, that is, surrounded by positive external factors alone, doesn't do us any good anyway.

To feel good, we need the right balance and negative external factors are part of this balance; thus, they are necessary too.

Modern society's actions, however, are directed toward the eradication of all negative external factors, with the outcome that the resultant suffering, in the end, is worse because it is unjustified.

All of this makes us panic and rush to the doctor with the belief of being severely ill and in need of urgent medical attention:

I have no reason to feel bad + I suffer anyway =
I'm ill!

All of this is physiological, not pathological, and there is no medical treatment that can solve the problem; there are just mental and behavioural 'cures'.

Of course, if our mood issues are diagnosed as pathological, then it is necessary to avail ourselves of a suitable medical treatment; but if our issues aren't pathological, we have made the problem ourselves and must fix it: we need to become aware of it, understand it and obviously…

… change our behavior and lifestyle.

Happiness

How many people spend their lives seeking happiness? All of us. How many of them find it? No one. You can't find happiness because it doesn't exist: it's pure utopia.

And yet, we live with the belief that, sooner or later, there will be something in our lives that will finally make us happy forever.

We spend our lives seeking or waiting for this thing, without ever finding it because it doesn't exist.

This entails the creation of dreams, illusions and the conviction that we are unlucky, with frustration as the result.

We look at others thinking how happy and lucky they are, maybe just because they are wealthy or famous. We look at Prince Joe Public's or a famous actor's marriage, and we think how lucky they are because they have all that they need for a happy life: money, fame, success…

Ah, poor me, what a sad life! I am so unfortunate. Will I ever be happy one day, too?

Absolutely not, we are all in the same boat. No line will ever be constantly on the upper side of anyone's graph, because it's biologically impossible and we should just forget about it: our nature doesn't allow for it, suffering is physiological, and it is the same for everyone, it is impossible to escape.

(Happiness graph)

The mood function, and thus our sinusoid, is inexorable. We need to accept this and use it as is, in the best way possible.

Prince Joe Public, the famous actor and everybody else are not happy, despite apparently having all that they need to gain happiness. They are like the rest of us mere mortals: same graph, same positive and negative mood swings and thus the same frustrations; or rather, even worse frustrations, because they are deemed unjustified!

Anyway, this first serious error of interpretation – seeking something that doesn't exist – is followed by another, more serious mistake: attributing a specific cause to their hypothetical lack of happiness, even if 'the cause' has nothing to do with it.

The typical casualties of their witch hunt are essentially three: their partner, their job and the place where one lives . They convince themselves that they need to change one or all of them to gain the long-sought-after gold at the end of the rainbow, with the real risk of ending up worse than before.

We aren't always happy and that's normal and physiological. It's true for everyone.

Before we try to change our partner, our job or the place where one lives we should think well if they really are the problem or if the problem is within us. Of course, changing the former three is easier and quicker, while changing the fourth is a little difficult, if not impossible.

Anyway, good luck and be happy…
… As much as possible!

Crime News (Part Two)

Let's talk about crime news again and recall two tragic occurrences: a murder and a suicide out of love.

I have already said that love is incompatible with those acts; in fact, these actions are guided only by suffering, pain and one's compass having gone rogue. The resulting violent behaviour is primarily aimed at eliminating the perceived cause of one's suffering.

Let's analyse the murder: at first, there is the positive phase of a couple's relationship, with its heightened mood and sense of well-being; but this phase, as we all know, cannot last and this is why that the couple enters a crisis until they split up. At this point, the mood of the man collapses (also due to the mechanism of grief) and he has the erroneous conviction that the only cause of his suffering is the loss of his partner. Alas, she's unavailable now, or she's available for a different man; and that's when distress and jealousy spike, thus generating a mix of severe psychological suffering, selfishness, hate and revenge. All of this leads to anti-social behaviour like stalking or violence.

In the case of suicide, the story is similar: a profound suffering emerges with seemingly no end, followed by far-too-great a sorrow and the erroneous conviction that the pain will never end, since the only way to be happy is to be together with their partner.

Thus, they kill themselves to end their their suffering but also to get revenge. Am I suffering? Then you'll suffer too because of my action!

These actions are totally egotistical, and they lack love in any form. Let us think twice, or rather 142 times before acting in a certain way; one only needs to wait for it to pass, one only needs to wait for one's batteries to recharge and for one's mood to be restored.

Of course, if mood were to fall into the pathological sphere, into mood disorders, the problem is amplified and remains stable, and these could be precisely the cases in which violent and extreme acts are more likely, because the real problem (the mood disorder) is not recognized and is mistakenly attributed solely to one's partner, seen as the only cause of one's suffering but also as the only possible solution.

We should remember that there is no right person or, alternatively, there are a multitude of them, as maths and statistics tell us, hence we shouldn't fixate nor insist on seeking a specific person because it's just an illusion and a volatile dream. The world is full of opportunities.

First of all, we need to learn to be happy on our own, to live and coexist with ourselves, to be autonomous and not depend on anything and anyone. We should learn to be enough for ourselves and to reject the absolute need of having someone else beside us.

This doesn't mean excluding the rest of the world or a partner, of course, but they shouldn't be essential or vital. A partner shouldn't complete us: we should do it ourselves.

Concrete autonomy is the best choice to live well and be ready for a real, serious and long-lasting relationship with someone else.

> "If a person is in love with you and needs to be with you, let them be.
> If a person is not in love with you, does not need to be with you but wants to be with you, hold them close"

If you want to stop suffering because of love, you just need to wait a little bit, put aside your dreams, illusions and seek the truth.

Only truth never betrays: it's our true friend and a trustworthy partner, it alone can help us…

… And, if you want it, it's always there.

Progress

How did people live in the past? Has progress brought good or evil into the world? Are we better or worse off than before? Have our lives improved? Are we humans happier for all our technological?

Apparently, the answers are obvious: of course, men are happier and their lives have improved; everything has changed with progress and people are better off than before. What a foolish question!

Are we sure about that? Are we sure that we are better off and happier than before? Are we living the lives we want and deserve?

Culture, science and technology have given us great tools to live better, and this is undeniable. Are we using them well, though?

Maybe. We have already spoken about our mood swings: that it continuously goes up and down and periods of well-being alternate with periods of distress, and that's inevitable.

The worst kind of suffering, however, is the unjustified and unmotivated one, being sick without a real reason. It would be better if a slump in mood was associated with a concrete or tangible issue in our lives, there being a real, motivating cause or difficulty that we could define as 'physiological'.

Those justified slumps in mood would alternate with equally physiological, natural spikes that would also be motivated, concrete and real. This alternating dynamic of our curve and especially the coherence between mood and life would lead humans to live in a balanced, physiological way.

Do we live like this in our technological age?

Absolutely not, because in a prosperous society there is no concrete, tangible and physiological reason that could justify a slump in our mood; they have all been struck off and labelled as unconceivable and un-acceptable.

This is unlike in the past, when those reasons were clearly commonly and concretely present; and all of this in an environment that was difficult and beautiful at the same time, fascinating, natural and with significantly more relaxed rhythms of life.

Those 'healthy' and 'physiological' difficulties of life, related to a decline in mood, would then enhance the positive moments that were equally motivated, tangible and natural. In this way, the mood sinusoid had wider range, was dynamic and reflected what happened in real life, there being complete harmony between mood and environment.

Well-being has eliminated the objective and healthy justifications for our physiological suffering, and that alone is a problem, but it has also eliminated the strategies useful for soothing this suffering, which are linked to our behavior, because luxuries and comforts have reduced—or even nullified—the need for action, and this contributes significantly to preventing us from feeling truly well.

It could be argued that life was objectively worse in the past: it was harsher and more difficult, but the mood curve was more dynamic and coherent. Nowadays our lives are objectively better, there's greater potential for happiness, but there also is the risk of illness, unhappiness and restlessness, as our incoherent mood curves tends to flatten. Seeking a solution to this situation isn't easy because it's connected to our way of life, and that needs to change.

We should ask ourselves if it would be better to return to a past way of life, with its difficulties and deprivations, that we seem to need in order to be happy.

No, thank-you; we should exclude this option in advance, given everything that we have achieved throughout the last centuries. However, in some respects, we need to recover at least the 'style' of past times.

We worry so much about future generations that will have to live without the advantages of fossil fuels, but I think there could be no better gift than to quickly be done with that damned 'black gold'. I envy those people who will be able to go back to calmer, more natural and human-centred lives, while at the same time still enjoying the benefits of modern science and technology. The rhythms of life will be more measured and people will be healthier and happier.

How lucky they will be! We could be too, now…

… But we are too dumb and lazy to change!

The Lottery

To be or to have? There's no doubt that the prevailing message of our society is the will and desire to 'have' (one just needs to look around to perceive it); meanwhile, the will and desire to 'be' are much less obvious.

Now, it's easy to judge and be self-righteous, to lay blame and seek solutions, but the truth is that that's the way we are. It's in our nature, and this isn't without justification because the will 'to have' feeds our stomach, the will 'to be' less so.

This approach, however, also entails the common illusion that the possession of money and material goods can help everybody achieve that long-strived for happiness, deemed unachievable through other earthly means. We have already seen that the pursuit of happiness is a pure utopia, but the same applies to the misconception that happiness comes from material goods!

While money isn't on the list inside your pocket, since it issn't among the things that make us feel good, at the same time, the act of engaging in gainful employment, in fact, increases our emotional well-being; that's why so many people gamble hoping to become millionaires.

I could understand it if they didn't have a shred of economic freedom, or if they were homeless or without a job, with a family to provide for, as in that case a small win would surely be both right and appropriate; but the majority of people that gamble have a house, a job, a car and a family, not seeming to realise how lucky they are when pursuing the mirage of easy money.

Let's try to analyse the hypothetical trend of the lucky winner's mood. How might a big win influence him? Would it increase his mood for a few days? For a week, maybe?

Yes, for sure, but then his emotional barometer would go back to the way it was before. It would increase and decrease, as if nothing had happened. When the brief moment of euphoria had passed, what would the winner think about?

'But how? I finally have everything I ever wanted, the dream of my life. I'm the luckiest man: I don't have to work because I have so much money, I can afford my dream house and amazing cars. I can travel whenever I want, but I'm not as happy as I thought. Heck! Am I sick, perhaps?'

He would miss his job, and that's really important for the balance of his mood, both as a positive and as a negative factor. Moreover, money makes one happy when one earns it, surely not when one just possesses it, and it makes one extremely unhappy when one loses or spends of it. Someone who wins a lot of money is skipping the only phase that could give him a little happiness and gratification, leaving just the 'neutral' possession and especially the 'depressive' and continuous loss of it.

What about friends and relatives? When they find out about the winnings, they will suddenly become affectionate and the winner will find himself having to defend himself against them.

Perhaps he will be disappointed because his mood is the same as before but with no dreams left, because they are either achievable or have already been achieved; and it's the dreams that makes us alive, not their fulfilment!

The winner, alone like a dog, will spend his days losing money and trying to defend himself and his winnings against everything and everyone. In this context of boredom and depression, he will end up with an irreparably ruined life. And all of this with the real possibility that he will lose everything, suddenly finding himself broke, something that often happens to the winners of big wins, who are unable to manage them.

Indeed, the lottery only gives joy to people who just dream about their victory, and gives sorrow to people that truly win; thus, the losers win, because they don't experience disillusion, and the winners lose, because they have to come to terms with a reality that will surely disappoint them.

It's fine to gamble and to dream, but if you discover you have won the lottery…

… Throw away the ticket away or give it to charity!

Heating and Mood

Hi! Good to see you. How are you?

§ Oh my God, there you go again. You're about to enlighten me about something again, aren't you?

You want to tell me, affirm or theorise that my mood could depend on the heating system of my house, even to a small extent? Four pipes, radiators and a boiler? Ha, ha, ha… You're so funny!

Yes, that's right. It could depend on that: a new, expensive and technologically advanced heating system. Sit down and listen to me.

Let's analyse two different families: the first one, my family, lives in a house with a fully automated gas heating system. Each room is independently regulated, with its own thermostat, and each hour a specific temperature is set. All of this does not require the slightest physical or mental effort. I don't even need to pay my bills: my bank takes care of them.

Oh, how nice! What luxury! How wonderful this convenience is!

The second family, on the other hand, uses the firewood they find in the forest to keep warm: they need to take care of the forest and to cut, collect, transport and store the firewood. Every day they fill the stove, light it and tend the fire. What an effort all this work is, and despite the physical and mental stress they only get an unsteady and uncontrolled temperature.

Right, how do you think the two different domestic situations influence those people's mood? Who's going to feel better? Who's going to feel happier and more gratified?

Which is better: the modern style that doesn't require any direct effort or struggle to that end (I still need to work), or the past style that is exhausting, challenging and which gives mixed results, but, at the same time, is well targeted and substantial?

It's easy for us to answer, now that we are experts in the field: between the two, the family that worked hard, built, strove and suffered to obtain something that is substantial and tangible will be and feel satisfied. These are all negative and positive 'physiological' factors that we need to stay at our peak: effort, struggle, hard work, fulfilment, gratification and satisfaction.

Warming up will never be a problem or a cause for concern for the first family, but it will also never be a source of pleasure or satisfaction (flat mood).

The second family will be gratified by what they have built and will be satisfied with the result. They will see it as a good opportunity to synchronise their mood curve with their real lives, thus managing to make it more dynamic, something that the first family will be unable to do, since warming up to them is absolutely sterile, taken for granted and thus devoid of emotion, good or bad as these may be.

This is only a small example related to domestic life, but we could give many more of them. They might even appear trivial and unimportant, taken individually; but if they're taken and added together, they become much more important due to their accumulative positive effect on our mood

Modern life and its comforts deprive us of the small but authentic struggles and battles that are the spice of life and that make us feel really great, often with little effort.

Drug-addicted and Love-sick

This association might appear odd and unlikely, and yet there are some affinities between the two categories that concern, guess what, exactly the mechanisms of our mood.

The drug addict is in fact a 'sick' person in need of help and care to soothe his suffering; unfortunately, he chose the wrong way to heal: the use of an exogenous and self-prescribed chemical substance to escape his suffering, as if this treatment is a valid alternative to official medicine.

What about the smitten man? Is he a drug addict too? Of course he is, and he became one without his knowledge; however, the chemical substances he uses unknowingly aren't exogenous and toxic, but endogenous, healthy and natural. What? A physiological drug? A healthy drug?

That is right. We ourselves are the makers and consumers of this fantastic drug that is absolutely clean, legal and accepted by everyone, even our grandmothers!

Just like the exogenous drug, however, this drug has huge limitations and flaws: price, dependence and addiction, with the real possibility, at any moment, of withdrawal symptoms if things really conk out the moment the couple falls apart . We call this love sickness for a reason.

The crisis happens when you're addicted and receive a lower amount of the chemical substance you were (mis)using: your mood slumps and your sinusoid moves to the depression zone for a long period of time. This crisis affects both soul and body with an unspeakable pain that seems to have no possible cure, it is primarily based on the grief mechanism caused by the loss of a loved one

During this time, the love-sick man thinks: 'Well, only now, while suffering, have I finally understood that she was the woman of my dreams, my true love, and that I can't live without her.'

In reality, the strong feeling within him isn't love, but his suffering, and since his sinusoid is in an extremely negative regressive zone, the only reason he wants to get back with his lover is to stop his pain, nothing else.

In order not to suffer, the drug addict looks for his usual dose from a trustworthy dealer. The love-sick man, instead, struggles to get better because he can't easily find the 'goods' he needs. The shortest route would be to make peace with his partner or find a different one, but it's complicated. His only other alternative is to be alone and suffer, waiting that the biochemical mechanisms of mood rearrange themselves to a new balance. During this situation of abstinence, the couple goes through a typical on and off period, characterised by three distinct phases:

1) They break up because they aren't happy together any more, with the belief that there's no love between them (addiction).

2) When they are alone, however, they feel worse and believe the opposite (abstinence and grief).

3)They get back together and, after a really short period of relative comfort (since the chemical substances kick in again in an organism that was finally about to head toward freedom), everything is back as before: 'You know, I thought that... I believed... But I was wrong... I'm confused...'

In the end, the couple has two choices: give in and resign themselves to their fate, with the inexorable flattening of their mood curves...

... Or change their 'dealer'!

Danger, Fear and Mood

In every human action, there's always some form of risk; in fact, there's always the possibility to harm ourselves or others.

Of course, the risk depends on the type of activity: there are high-risk activities and low-risk activities; some of them are safer, others are less so.

Saying that a specific activity is safe might be misleading: 'safe' means that there's a low risk for a negative event to happen, but it doesn't mean that the event will never happen, as we typically think. Moreover, the degree of risk doesn't concern only the likelihood that the event itself will happen, but also its real and concrete consequences (like with nuclear power plants).

Danger causes a reaction of fear, that is a function of our body, associated with a lower mood. This function exists to prevent any potentially harmful behaviour and it's an innate mechanism, as are many of our fears; we can also acquire new fears through life, coming from our and other people's life experiences.

Some fears have to be innate, like the fear of venomous snakes or of falling off a cliff; in fact, personal experience would be perfectly useless in such cases.

It is correct to fear dangerous activities because it's useful and healthy; on the other hand, fearing nondangerous activities, as is the case of phobias, doesn't serve any purpose and it might even be a serious problem.

If humans evolved with congenital and good fears that should guide them to behave correctly, why do they often take part in dangerous activities that not only elicit fear but are also perfectly useless?

For example, some people reach the top of a mountain climbing a grade VII path instead of taking a nearby and safer route that reaches the same mountain top.

Why do they risk their safety without any real and concrete advantage? All of this isn't convenient from an evolutionary point of view and is also therefore apparently illogical and stupid. Why, then? *Homo stupidus*?

The answer is simple for us almost *on-off* beings: because we really like doing dangerous things and they make us feel great; because risking our necks really spikes our mood.

'I could have taken the normal path to the top, of course, and I would have enjoyed it too, but when I take the VII grade climb, my mood spike is much higher. Experiencing is believing!'

All of this is senseless, however, because it is counterproductive for the individual and indeed the entire community; *Ergo*, there's no advantage for the human species.

Maybe the fear mechanism doesn't work correctly in those people? Maybe it wasn't selected in a just and balanced way? Maybe Nature messed up this time?

Actually, it's just a matter of time. Natural selection is an ongoing process because environment and genetics are continuously and casually evolving; this means that no one will ever be a perfect being at a specific time and in a specific environment. We will always be *too late*.

Natural selection never ends and exists right now; only the best, the strongest and the most cautious survive.

§ Wait! Earlier you said that fear is associated with a decrease in mood; how does it make you feel good, then?

The fear mechanism works in two distinct and succeeding phases. The first phase modulates behaviour, discouraging you from performing potentially dangerous actions, and it's called the damage prevention phase; the second phase, linked to the first one, helps you when you're already in a dangerous condition, stimulating your body and your psyche to allow you to succeed.

If you happen to come across a bear on a trail, fear causes you to freeze, but it also prepares the high performance required for a possible defence or, more likely, an escape.

The biochemical mechanisms necessary to increase *performance* have a side effect: the increase of our mood. In addition to this, there also is the *rebound* effect of the first negative phase (the damage prevention phase), which increases our mood even more. You know, it's a godsend!

It's the second phase that makes us feel good and it's the same phase we look for, wittingly or unwittingly.

To many people, the first phase is enough to avoid specific dangerous action, while to other people this phase is surmountable and lets them reach the second phase, with its stimuli, satisfaction and pleasure! This is why people invented and keep inventing a myriad of *senseless* risky and dangerous activities, like extreme sports.

Amusement parks with their thrilling attractions and roller coaster rides simulate dangerous activities: fear reigns supreme, but there's no real danger that could threaten our safety, at least one hopes not.

We think about, look for and do dangerous activities because they make us feel good and appease and gratify us, despite all the risks involved.

For many people this benefit far exceeds fear and its risks. It is in all respect a potentially harmful and addictive drug, which many can't possibly do without. We could consider it a 'risk addiction'.

Among the various and classic dangerous activities for a select few, like climbing, skydiving, etc., there is one that is easily accessible, practical (you just need to sit) and available to everyone: car- or motorbike-racing at full speed.

Again, the mechanism is simple and is a cascade mechanism: speed means risk, risk means fear, fear means the increase of our mood.

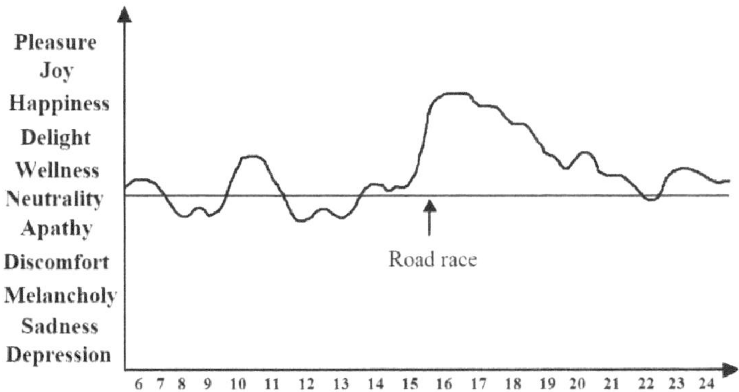

We race with our cars or motorcycles in order to feel good, happier and more excited: one just needs to press the throttle a bit more and, as if by magic, one feels more alive!

Speed is used as a medicine, as a drug or as an anti-depressant, but it can also have serious collateral effects.

We should avoid these kinds of reckless activities that are a potential danger to ourselves and others, and always remember that there are healthier ways to increase our mood!

§ Like sex, drugs and rock 'n' roll?

Well… I mean… My list was different, a little longer and more sober, but… Just take out drugs, at least!

Anyway, let's try not to be stupid and hurt ourselves and the others, because we only have one life to live and nothing else…

… Thus, it's better to follow the footpath and respect the speed limits.

Drugs and Alcohol

Every one of us is always looking for their own physical and psychical well-being. There are many different natural, healthy and physiological methods to obtain this result (the list); in addition to them, however, people have discovered some unnatural and even execrable shortcuts that are intended to obtain a similar effect, but they also amplify and distort them.

These unnatural shortcuts are called 'drugs' and 'alcohol'. I have separated them into two categories out of habit, but we should consider alcohol a fully fledged drug. To complete the picture, let me add caffeine, nicotine and psych meds to the same category: they are all chemical and exogenous substances that artificially affect our psychic functions and our mood, being addictive.

To be clear, if you see someone on the street smoking a cigarette, he or she is consuming a dose of nicotine, out in the open and without any shame; on par with any junkie getting his fix in the park.

If someone drinks a guiltless aperitif at a bar, in reality they are getting a dose of alcohol in order to obtain a specific pharmacologically induced effect of peace, well-being and serenity, and not just because the aperitif tastes good and is refreshing. Everyone, in their own home, can 'get a fix' of psych meds, in a legal way.

These are all different kinds of behaviour with the same purpose, and they are legal, widespread and accepted by everybody through habit; they are also only apparently innocent and harmless. They amount to a fully fledged consumption of drugs, and sometimes it's not the type of substance that makes the difference, but the quantity.

If a nation decides to prohibit the use and commercialisation of drugs, it should prohibit all of them, without distinction, or, it should legalise all of them; there's no in between because it makes no logical sense.

Are you familiar with the cocoa plantations in South America? Or the vineyards outside our homes?

They are the same: producers of chemical substances that alter our psyche, improve our mood and cause addiction. Just try to sell alcohol-free wine. Best of luck!

Now, the possibility of increasing our mood whenever and however we want by simply getting these substances, is clearly tempting. The result is guaranteed and more amplified compared to the physiological one. What could be better than that…
It's nice to go out with friends, knowing that you'll have fun and feel great; you just need to assume a chemical substance and everything is guaranteed: an awesome night out and equally awesome highs.

'What a wonderful evening! First an aperitif, then a

night out with wine, beer and cocktails! Guaranteed fun!' Are you having fun because of your friends or the alcohol, though?

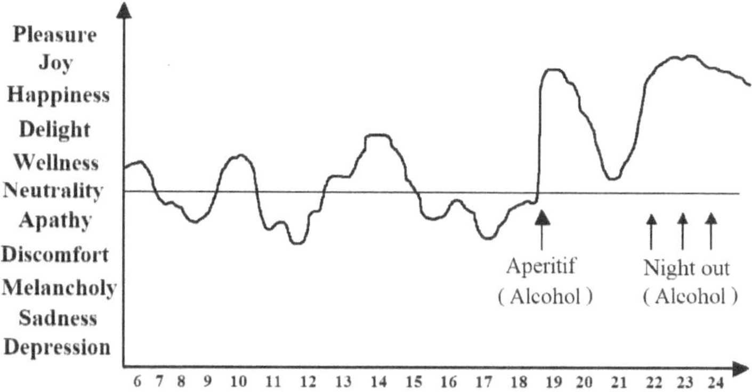

An artificial increment of your mood will never be as pleasant as the physiological and natural one, though. It might be more intense, that's true, but not better. Moreover, after the increase there's always a subsequent decrease (*rebound* effect): a strong decrease corresponds to a strong increase, and if the decrease is not associated with anything tangible or concrete that might justify it, significant discomfort is guaranteed.

The problem becomes dramatic when you become totally addicted to those substances: at some point, you don't need them to feel good but just not to feel bad. In this way, all physiological and natural mechanisms of mood regulation stop working: farewell compass; farewell list; farewell behavioural guidelines. The principal aim of our existence becomes the acquisition and daily consumption of chemical substances.

You might avoid becoming a real drug addict, but if you always look for chemical substances to have fun with your friends, then something is wrong.

You can enjoy your friends, good music and beautiful girls or guys at the disco; that's enough and you shouldn't look for anything else because you don't need it. You already have all the ingredients needed to have fun and feel good (today and tomorrow, too).

Always remember that you can even do double somersaults, but the balance of your 'mood account' will always be zero in the end; this is why you should try to obtain the same result without doing yourself harm and destroying body and mind.

You know, dude, we have to be smart…

… Ah, you're smart already? Well, then you need to
be smarter still!

Coffee

Coffee is really good! I adore it and love its flavour and its flagrance; drinking it is a real pleasure that affects the body and the soul.

I like cola, too: so fresh and all those bubbles. It's thirst quenching and there's no comparison with any other soft drinks (maybe they're missing something...)

But is this really the case? Do we drink coffee just because it's good and cola because of its thirst-quenching properties?

I think that something helps their commercial success: this something is called caffeine, a chemical substance that causes positive effects on our mood and physical and mental performance. What do you think happens after you drink a good cup of coffee?

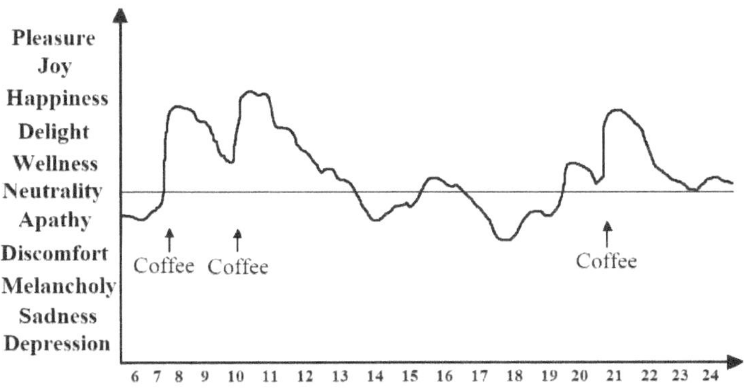

Our mood improves and our sinusoid goes up, with a certain and always reproducible result. When the effect of coffee wears off, obviously, mood decreases and thus it's time for another coffee.

Maybe we don't realise it, but the real reason why we drink coffee is because it makes us feel good, and the fact that it is also really good – and I agree with that – is of secondary importance.

'So, what do you say? How about a coffee?'

You already know that you'll feel good because coffee recharges you and improves your mood.

'I feel a bit down and suffer an existential dullness… Come on, let's drink some coffee.'

And you already know you'll surely feel great.

You can become coffee-addicted, or addicted to a chemical and exogenous substance that modifies your mood, and thus to a fully fledged drug, even if it's light and harmless in normal doses.

Moreover, caffeine is a stimulant and after the stressful and fast-paced lives we already live, we don't really need another stimulus; if anything, a good camomile would be much more useful.

Anyway, any exogenous substance that artificially increases our mood isn't good in principle.

We are talking of caffeine; what about nicotine?

It's the same mechanism, but compared to coffee, cigarettes have devastating effects on our health and our wallet!

It's insane to spend money just to harm ourselves, and yet it happens, because it's the chemical substance dictates the norm, not us.

Very well, now I'm feeling a bit tired…
… Let me get a coffee!

Football

The game of football and its associated fans are one of the weirdest and most irrational phenomena of our society. It's spread all over the world and has hooked millions of people; alas, myself included.

It's irrational because you can't justify the huge amount of time, energy and effort that fans devote to something so far removed from their lives; in fact, it has nothing to do with them!

Fans put their heart and soul into watching this sport: they know everything about their team, the players and the championship, constantly informed by newspapers, TV and *social networks*.

What commitment! What an effort! What devotion!

Do those fans ever realise that the team they idolise doesn't really care about them and their ordinary, little lives?

Then why do they still insanely and irrationally love them? Why do they perpetuate a devotion that is never reciprocated? *Homo stupidus*?

Anyway, teen girls used to scream and cry during the Beatles' concerts. Do you think the four singers cared about them?

There's more: you just need to delve into the topic to find out how irrational the choice of a particular team is. Why this team and not that one? Why them in particular? Hell, they might even belong to a different city!

Often the choice has no logic or rationale, no justification nor real or concrete motivation to justify it. Usually, the phenomenon starts during one's childhood, grows stronger year after year and might even remain unchanged for the rest of one's life!

Usually, the choice of a team is guided by a long-term supporter (a friend, an uncle, a cousin); from then on, you follow the path set out for you blindly, without wondering too much about why or how you made that choice in the first place.

It almost seems a form of religious belief, a blind faith that is closed to reason.

In the case of religion, however, the answer is simpler: you follow one because you're born into it and, inevitably, you are brought up in it without choice. In the case of football, at least you could choose freely between several teams.

If you ask people the reason why they support a specific team, they will always reply: 'Because they are the strongest! They are the best! They are the only real team!'

You get similar answers if the question is related to religion: 'Because it's the real one! Because it's the right one! Because… Are there any others?'

The latter answers are right and acceptable, because faith is blind by definition: it would be absurd to have faith in a God that taps on your shoulder and tells you:

'Hey, I'm right here!' What kind of faith would that be?

Football, however, can't work like that. These answers are not enough! There must always be a logical and concrete reason why you root for one team, a reason that justifies your choice, because football is not a religion.

One could even swap all the players on the team, including its coach, and it wouldn't matter to the fan: his favourite team would be the same and he would still call it the best and the strongest.

If there were at least some form of loyalty (if, for example, only Milanese players were members of A.C. Milan and only Milanese fans rooted for them; similarly, if only Florentine players were members of A.C.F. Fiorentina and only Florentine fans rooted for them; and so on…), then yes, I could find a little bit of logical justification. It would be similar to fans rooting for their national football team.

Now, it is legitimate to ask why people have such blind faith and won't listen to reason. Once again, however, the answer is simple: we have already seen that we humans need dreams to increase their mood and hence to feel good; it's fine to be on the look out for mood-changers, as long as it's for the better. Unfortunately, to do this, it's necessary to make a commitment; it requires willingness to get involved, and the results are not always either brilliant or certain.

People, as we know, are lazy and always look for shortcuts to save time and expend minimal effort. This paves the way for imagination and the search for emotional highs while sitting on the couch with a remote in hand. Those emotions are external to our lives and have nothing to do with us really, but we adopt them anyway.

Our lives doesn't satisfy us enough? Then we dream of other people's lives and live their emotions and dreams as if they were ours; we adopt them and feel them.

For the same reason, we read celebrity magazines dreaming of other people's lives and loves, but we also dream when we simply watch a good film, a tv series, read a good book or, indeed, read The *Sport's Gazette!*

These are other people's emotions and we make them our own to get a cheap thrill, but in the end, fortunately or unfortunately, we make do with what we have.

This doesn't mean that we should close stadiums, theatres, cinemas, etc. On the contrary, they are welcome, but we should look for them in the right and balanced proportion, diversifying our interests as much as possible.

We and our healthy and genuine emotions should have top priority; even if they seem less exciting, they are certainly better than the artificial and colourful emotions administered to us (and that could even completely replace them) that in fact don't really exist...

… Thus, long live my life and then long live Inter!

"Teaching only one religion at a young age
is a serious mistake, a form of violence,
which inevitably brings severe consequences.
All religions should be taught
and given equal weight;
it is then up to the individual, upon reaching maturity,
to freely decide which one to follow,
or to follow none at all"

Food

What will always be the simplest, most convenient and most available method to increase our mood? The answer is simple for us simple beings: food. You only need to look around a little to understand that, because it's difficult to hide those extra pounds.

On the other hand, not surprisingly, food is one of our essential needs, together with water and sex, in descending order of importance and need. What are you saying, you males? Sex should be in the first place?

Then just try not to drink, eat and have sex for a week. If you are still alive, walk into a room where there is a cold beer, a tasty pizza and a *super girl* waiting with impatience.

What do you think will be your sequence of fulfilment? Drinking, eating and then having sex, that's for sure, in order of vital importance.

Usually we have plenty of water, sex is a rare and complex commodity while food is easily accessible, available and with the best cost-benefit ratio.

What's better than eating something good like chips, peanuts, sweets or chocolate to improve your mood when you are out of sorts? You don't need to be really hungry to get this result; even the simple action of thinking or talking about it or expecting it can make you feel better.

Of course, this kind of fulfilment is inexorably registered and made visible to everyone in the form of fat memory, and thus your aesthetic and health problems begin.

There are people that exacerbate this behaviour, making food their main or unique purpose in life and neglecting everything else, just like real drug addicts.

We eat to feel good and we make dinner reservations because it makes us feel good, and if we do it in good company everything becomes even better because we are in front of a double positive factor.

Let's try another test now. It's evening, you are really hungry and there are three different options available to you: skipping dinner, eating alone or eating with someone else. These are the results:

1) Skipping dinner   (0%) Sadness
2) Eating alone   (10%) Well-being
3) Eating with someone else (90%) Happiness

On average, the third choice is the winning one because, in fact, it makes us feel really great and increases our mood much more than the other two, and this is our real aim, not the food or the company.

Food makes us happy, that's true, but we shouldn't exaggerate the amount we eat because it should satisfy us mentally, not physically, and this satisfaction depends on its quality, deliciousness, tastiness and palatability, not on its absolute quantity.

§ What do you mean? The more I eat, the happier I am. It's mathematical!

Wrong! If you want to be mentally satisfied, you shouldn't eat like a pig but opt instead for good and tasty food, always in the right amount and without exceeding…

… Anyway, enjoy your meal!

Reality and Fantasy

We should never take anything too seriously in life, especially ourselves. We have to be able to laugh and smile at ourselves, our limits and our flaws.

We only have one life, never to be repeated and we should try to live it in a constructive and balanced way, and for what it really is; the important thing is not to understand what life truly is, but to understand what it isn't.

In this way, we immediately eliminate the existential problem and thus the problem of the meaning and purpose of our existence, or rather, of the universe, since we are a direct consequence of it.

This purpose or motivation doesn't exist at all and isn't anywhere. It's not like we aren't smart enough to find or understand it, but it simply isn't there and looking for it – we are masters at this – is a fun exercise that won't ever bring any results.

If the universe had a purpose and a reason to exist, it would need something above it that could, in fact, justify it. We could even accept that, but this 'something' would have no purpose or reason to exist either. Thus, the existential problem would be the same, unless it too had something above it which could further justify it.

In the end, the basic issue is just moved one level up, or rather, the basic issue does not exist because we invented it from scratch.

IPSE DIXIT

It's convenient for us to solve our existential problem by appealing to the existence of God's.

It's easy to place this heavy burden on his shoulder, poor guy, as if he didn't have enough troubles.

Very well! We have finally solved our problem and can live peacefully. You can deal with it, you can sort it out, since you're so creative!

Sometimes I wonder if he too invented something above Himself that could give him peace of mind and justify his existence"

Thus, we shouldn't worry too much about ourselves and the world. Let's not make life more difficult and, more importantly, not be afraid of people's criticism because what they say is just a lot of hot air anyway.

What we are, what we think and what we say doesn't matter to anyone; we all are too selfish to care about anyone else's life, so we shouldn't feel judged by anyone because they aren't really judging us.

§ What are you talking about? If someone speaks ill of me, and thus judges me, shouldn't I take it seriously? Shouldn't I react?

No, because everyone speaks ill of everyone else, and you do the same; the point is not to misjudge any specific person, but, by reflex, to only speak well of yourself.

We are simple, foolish and stupid animals and we shouldn't be afraid, or indeed ashamed to admit it. Good or bad, all of us are. That's life; we are made like that and we function like that. There's no fault, much less any solutions.

Let's debunk the intelligence myth, because it has no value. A smart person isn't worth more than a person who is less smart. Being smart is like getting very muscular: it can be useful, that's true, but it has no value. People's true values are frankness, generosity, kindness and honesty. These values make the difference and we should look for them within the people that we want next to us.

§ What about self-confidence? That's really important! Everybody says that.

Enough about self-confidence! Why? Because its another lie we tell ourselves to feel good and be accepted by others. Yet another wobbly fantasy with its head in the clouds? Our beautiful but unstable house of cards?

We need to accept our lack of self-confidence serenely, feeling free to tell everybody about it, ourselves included, without any fear or shame, proud of our limits, weaknesses and flaws because it is these that make us human and give us our uniqueness and sense of being alive.

We must accept ourselves just as we are, without wanting to prove the opposite to ourselves or others, often grasping at straws.

Let's accept our merits and flaws, our positive and negative sides, as well as those of the people close to us, because no one chooses to be what they are or is at fault because of it.

Humans are simple and predictable beings that depend on a few basic rules to govern their behaviour; despite this advantage, they have managed to complicate everything, including their lives, because they have irreparably moved away from reality with all their fantasy and creativity. Reality has been replace by *fantasy*, causing incalculable damage.

Let's think about the three main things upon which all of us usually base our lives: most of our behaviour revolves around **religion**, **relationships** and **material goods**, for better or for worse. They are at the basis of our three biggest lies, our amazing *fantasy*, because we don't experience them for what they really are. We have cleverly changed and distorted their meaning and importance.

Thus, we should deflate all the lies and fantasies in which we are immersed and which affect our lives so heavily. To do this, we must return to simple things:

nature, love and the ABCs of life, without pretty frills or other embellishments; we must live without *fantasy*.

To paraphrase Thoreau:

Rather than love, than money, than faith,
than fame, than justice…
Give me truth!

To paraphrase someone else (the amazing Caterina Caselli…)

The truth hurts you know …

The first quote is excellent, while the second one is wrong: truth always hurts less than a lie. Truth can really hurt in the short term, but it's a limited pain because you can understand and overcome it. Lies are insidious and they hurt less in the short term, but their pain can last forever.

It's better to comprehend that we only have one life and we should live it to the full, instead of believing in the illusion of eternity, thus risking spending our lives waiting.

It's better to live knowing that we'll never meet the people we love again when they die, instead of believing in the illusion of meeting them again, never finding closure. False illusions can be nice and comforting, but they only give us uncertainty, insecurity and anxiety; only truth can lead us to well-being, balance, understanding and peace, even if it's less exciting than lies.

Truth makes us feel good and at peace with the world, for better or for worse, including during difficulties and suffering.

'Truth, first, always, as our friend and trustworthy partner of life and existence; then everything else, then everyone else, then what's left. It's only in this way that the human machine can function at its best.'

Conclusions about Love

As we have seen, love is a great and noble sentiment, but it has no place in a couple's relationship, because Nature didn't consider it necessary. It only exists in our sparkling fantasy and if and when it is present, we can only find it in a minimal form, mixed up and regularly confused with our disruptive moods.

Indeed, there is a similarity between love and mood: both words have only four letters!

(In Italian language: Amore e Umore)

Maybe we should replace them with other words? Or we might use the right word in the right place.

Hello, my dear. I truly have a kind of love for you… I mean, a kind of mood for you. Goodbye, my love… Or rather, goodbye, my mood.

Yes, that would be better! Do you remember the song:

I defended, I defended, my love…

It should be:

I defended, I defended, my mood…

There's nothing to laugh about here: this is reality and this is the truth, but at the same time, I'm sure that the second version wouldn't have been very successful!

Sadly, the powerful magnet, glue and driving force that makes us meet and stay together isn't love, and that's why we must deflate all the unsustainable and unquenchable lies, fantasies and expectations that can only lead us to chronic dissatisfaction.

How many love poems, how many romantic novels and films? But they aren't true, they are fiction. They are just mood poems, mood novels and mood films; yes, our mood. Love is something else!

The fact that a couple's relationship is based on dreams and fantasies, in addition to mood, is due to the simple fact that the human race is opportunistic and is governed by tight deadlines: we should never forget that we only live for a few years; thus, we have little time, and dreams and fantasies are effective and most importantly short lived.

That which is created in every couple is always a fantastic yet unstable and precarious cocktail. At first it makes everything work in an excellent way, but then inevitably the whole thing blows up because the mechanism of non-truth cannot last forever. It's an unstable mechanism by definition.

§ If it cannot last … then is the mechanism faulty by definition?

No, because by the time the castle collapses, copulation has already taken place; thus, the mechanism holds up very well from an evolutionary perspective. It's fast, safe and well tested.

In this case, the mechanism of truth would have been a complete failure, a resounding fiasco, and indeed it hasn't evolved in the human species.

§ Fine, I could accept all of this, but if everything you said is true, what can we do with this truth in relation to a couple and their lives together? Is it useful or not? Where do we act on it? What importance should e give it?

Our species can't survive with truth but only without it; with lies, however, life inevitably becomes complicated. What should we do, then? What about falling in love? What do we do with that? Should we give it up?

No, come on, we can't! Are you sure we would be better off without these 'sweet' lies? It's so nice to dream and let our thoughts fly above the clouds, while we build castles in the air! It's so nice to fall in love. What should we do? How should we behave?

The rule of truth always works and is universal, but there are some exceptions that prove the rule. This is exactly the case where we should adhere to the rules because dreams and reality have to coexist within a couple, and one does not exclude the other.

Truth is necessary, but should be applied in the right place at the right time. As to dreams, we need them too and they are essential to our lives.

We need balance. If you want to live well, you shouldn't take yourself too seriously but you also shouldn't make fun of yourself either; you need to be mindful but astute when it comes to your fantasy and imagination.

Thus, you can make fun of yourself, that's absolutely fine, but only up to a certain point; then you need to come out with the truth, and truth will pave your life with gold.

Have you fallen in love? Very well, no problem. Live it to the fullest, play with it and take it easy: it will only make you feel good. It's only the first part of a couple's relationship, the purely selfish one, and that's how you should experience it: like a game or a dream.

It's not love, as we all know, because love is something else and mood sets the rules, but let's keep it that way. It's just a beautiful moment of your life.

You don't need the truth in the first part of your relationship, you can push it aside; you know it's there and you can use it whenever you need. You should only use the truth to avoid making mistakes, hurting others or yourself and creating useless stress or suffering.

You need the truth in the second part of your relationship, instead: it's the altruistic phase, or the concrete and mature family phase. Only the truth can allow a family to grow in harmony, joy and serenity;

not dreams, false illusions and castles in the air.

Of course, this way of life is something else, and it surely is less beautiful and exciting, but it's still positive and concrete. You can dream when you need to dream, but you have to burst your bubble and be realistic at some point.

Consider the beginning of the relationship simply as a game, an exciting game that makes you happy and nothing more; you're just a happy person that is playing. You can call it 'love' and enjoy it as it is, even if it isn't love, but call it 'mood' when necessary and you'll see that you can't go wrong that way.

If a couple's love is just a game, no matter how good, are you giving it the right importance? The right weight? Is it in the right position inside your scale of values? How much is a good game worth, compared to everything else?

Anyone who gives love absolute importance and consequently places it first in their *top ten* is definitely mistaken. It's a mistake many make in good faith, following their heart or their instinct, thinking about their youth and the emotions they still want to feel.

It's a mistake, because the most important thing for us and our lives is ourselves, and we should give the greatest importance to what we are, think and do and then only to our dreams and desires; everything else comes after that, including love.

§ Thus, love rightly and honourably ranks second, doesn't it? A well-deserved silver medal? First ourselves and then love. It sounds right.

But it's wrong. Family already ranks second.

§ Ah, family! Indeed, it might be more important than my desire to live high on emotion, as I did when I was sixteen. You might be right, I admit it. What about someone without a family, though?

Well, in that case, second place is vacant, waiting to be filled, but it's already reserved because you usually start a family sooner or later: love itself will evolve into family, acquiring new importance and amplifying its role.

(I'd also like to reiterate that a family can be created even without children)

Of course, when love gives way to family, you can't find it *in loco,* inside our sweet little homes any more; that would be too easy, but Nature didn't want that. Nature planned different things that are much more adventurous for us; thus you either renounce love, with a small sacrifice, or you look for it somewhere else.

Let's say that we can award love a dignified wooden medal, thus, an honourable fourth position. Or perhaps even the fifth might work.

Well, you decide, but if you want to find the right balance in your life and live well, love surely can't be on the podium, that's for sure; otherwise, you're still living immersed in your *fantasy*, committing a serious mistake that will have drastic consequences on your equilibrium and future serenity.

Let's try to outline two different lists of possible values.

The first list, the correct one, gives peace and serenity to our lives and existence, because it's complete and everything is in the right order of importance.

The second list, on the other hand, is still potentially complete, but makes the mistake of establishing a wrong order of importance, and that's why it can never give you a serene, happy and fulfilling life.

	Right	**Wrong**
1°	Ourselves	Love
2°	Family	….
3°	….	….
4°	Love	….

The first list is typical of a man who thinks first about himself, with a little healthy selfishness, then about his family and finally about everything else, including love. That way, he lives a right and balanced life.

The second list is usually typical of the female gender, who often has the bad habit of ranking love in first place, basing a good part of their lives and existence on a risky bet, that is lost from the start.

That would not be the case if they have children; indeed, in that case, family would surely rank first, but only temporarily. This is a typical widespread mistake of the female gender too.

The second list doesn't sit well because it's not based on reality. You cannot live a balanced, fulfilling and happy life following that list, because no matter how exciting a game is, it should never occupy first place and overshadow all the other values that are much more important, real and concrete. With the second list, you can only live a life of endless disappointment.

Love shouldn't be on the podium, that's true, but it is also true that love is surely in first place on the list you have in your pocket, if you rank those actions that improve our mood in order of efficiency and effectiveness. That's why the mistake of putting love in first place at the top of our list of values is understandable, indeed it is only human. Thus, we need to be careful not to make this serious mistake.

Love is a powerful force that only a true *Jedi* can really control; it's so powerful that it can even annihilate everything: our values, our loved ones, our lives and ourselves. You might be able to live with just love, water and stale bread, but then you would have to give up everything else.

§ I'm sorry to interrupt you, but while I could accept – conditionally – not putting love in first place, family should always be in first place. It's always the most important thing.

No, this is not the case. Ranking family first is another mistake, because a family atmosphere is really important and it mainly comes from the well-being of its individual components: if the parents are well and happy, they create a healthier, more fun and more peaceful family atmosphere that has a positive impact on their children, who consequently are happy as well. Of course, the children would get less attention, but that's not a negative thing; on the contrary, it's not good to give excessive attention to one's children as it hinders their healthy development.

The same applies to a partner: a happy partner makes the other partner happy too, irrespective of the amount of time one spends with him or her.

If we want a happy couple or family, first we need to be happy ourselves; thus, we must always rank ourselves first, being able to fulfil and satisfy our passions, interests and desires (within the limits of what's possible, of course). A couple and a family are beautiful things, but they shouldn't be our prison.

As we know, two main factors make the couple bond, and they are two attractive forces: **love**, indeed, in the initial phase, and **family** then, as the evolution of love.

The love that transforms into a family could be compared to a staircase: at the very top we find unrequited love, which is the purest, most enduring, and noblest form of love (because it contains only dreams and the positive aspects of a relationship). But once that love is reciprocated, you take the first step downward (because the negative aspects of a relationship also begin to appear), and from there it is all downhill, a slow decline until, at the very bottom, you find the family. At the beginning of a relationship, what keeps the couple together is the sense of well-being, the uplift in mood; but later, when that effect unfortunately and inevitably fades, what truly keeps the couple together is the unconscious desire to avoid the harsh suffering of separation, the pain of loss. (I know this may not sound very poetic, but that is reality).

Between those factors there's a third one, that can always contribute to uniting the couple and that we haven't considered or explored yet. This factor is called **sex**.

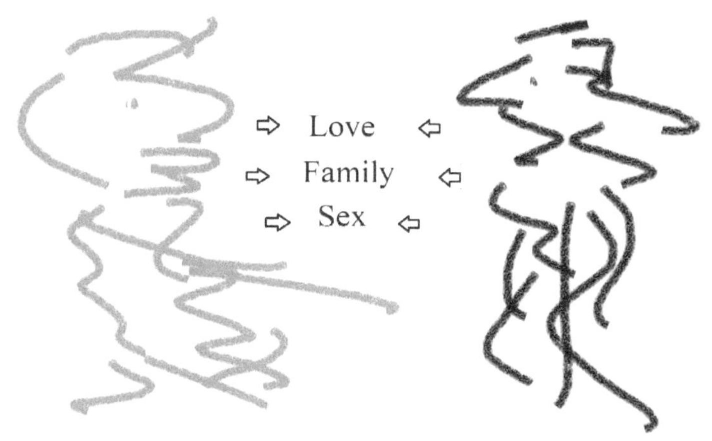

The third factor, sex, actively collaborates with the other two factors in making the couple bond; the three of them are absolutely necessary and fundamental for the survival of the human species.

While these three factors are usually associated, in reality each of them has a life of its own and its own reason for existing, and they could also be completely independent: you could fall in love with someone, have a family with someone else and have sex with a third person!

It could be possible if you only consider the laws of nature … Not with our laws, though!

'The best sex is without love,
the best love is without sex,
but together they get a better score!'

Let's summarise this in a diagram (I consider this indispensable! Relationships needs to be engineered to be understood!) to illustrate the possible association between the three factors that constitute this bond, (**L** for love, **F** for family and **S** for sex), and possible partners (**a**, **b**, **c**...).

We can put each possibility for each subject with the respective partner (or partners) inside square brackets. e.g.: [**L** with **a**] means 'love' with the partner 'a' and nothing else.

[**L** with **a**]　　[**F** with **a**]　　[**S** with **a**]　　[**LS** with **a**]

[**FS** with **a**]　　　[**F** with **a** + **S** with **b**]

[**FS** with **a** + **L** with **b**]　　　[**F** with **a** + **LS** with **b**]

[**FS** with **a** + **LS** with **b**]

[**F** with **a** + **L** with **b** + with **c**]

Etc.

Just like the alphabet, you might have more than three partners; in any case, however, it's not possible to associate **L** with **F** because **F** is always the evolution of **L**.

To prevent any misunderstanding, I'd like to clarify that the association between **L** and **F** could exist in nature, as it exists in fiction, because the laws of modern physics – not the laws of Galileo, though – allow it, but only at speeds close to that of light where the common concept of simultaneity of events vanishes.

Sadly, at this very moment and at sub-light speed, the first list – the correct one – is inapplicable because it is automatically prohibited by the laws we have made and that regulate every couple's relationship. According to these laws, indeed, family and love cannot coexist, because they are incompatible; therefore, we have to choose one of them or get to the root of the problem and change the laws themselves.

We have three possible choices:

1) **To give up love** and obtain everything else, which is no small thing, preserving family.

[**FS** with **a**] or [**F** with **a**]

1) **To give up family** and obtain love, but in this case, love would have to be continuously changed and redesigned, otherwise it would change into family over time.

[**L** with **a**] or [**LS** with **a**]

1) **To change the rules of the game**, modifying and updating the laws that regulate a couple's relationship, in order to allow a peaceful and long-lasting coexistence of family and even love, if we cannot do without it. [All of the above]

'Following several statistical tests, it was found that, when choosing between the three choices, the male gender chooses the third choice without hesitation. The female gender, instead, is more reluctant in expressing their free choice and they often assert their right not to answer, if their lawyer isn't present!'

To go through just the first two phases of a couple's relationship following the simple **L→F** sequence is currently normal and accepted by most people, but if the first phase **L** is not complete, then it's really difficult to maintain a peaceful second phase **F**, for a lifetime and till death do us part.

If the first phase is complete, it could even be sustainable: everything must be done at the right moment, though, because if you don't do them at the right moment, you'll do them later, even if it isn't the right moment any more. It's mathematical!

A braver alternative could be the double **L→F** sequence: to begin the second choice, **L**, when you're young, followed by a meticulous 'changing of the guard' at least every two years, so as to keep playing, feel good, and, most importantly, try to get as much experience as possible.

Then you can continue with **F**, family, and thus opt for the first choice, putting away your toy boxes and renouncing love for a while.

When the children are old enough and leave, and if your body and soul are still strong enough, then you can return to the second choice, **L**, dusting off the toy boxes and dreaming again... Or pretending to dream, at least.

Finally, the fourth and final step. As you grow old, you could return to the first choice, **F**, that would be the definitive one, finding peace and serenity again with your partner of a lifetime, growing older with them without regrets: at that point, indeed, you have already done all you had to do.

If you follow this pattern in your life, you could live two phases of love and two phases of family, that would be distinct and subsequent: **L→F→L→F**.

It's a normal, natural (and accepted) to start with **L**, love, and arrive at **F**, family. This isn't an absolute rule, though, and you could even start a relationship directly with **F**, thus being on good terms with the other person without falling in love with them and deciding, in good conscience and with your head on your shoulders, to start a family with them. There's nothing wrong with that; on the contrary, there could even be considerable advantages in terms of serenity and future stability, because the choice of a partner during the phase **L** can lack focus and thus not augur the brightest of futures, while you are much more aware and mindful during phase **F**!

Of course, if we go to the root of the problem with courage and confidence, in order to change those anachronistic laws that regulate our relationships, then all the previous examples, issues and complications will fade away. We would have open access to all of the previous associations all of the time and indulge ourselves. Anyway, that's another story!

Very well, at this point and after these premises, my dear girls (or boys; it's the same, because of the couple's transitive nature), beautiful and magnificent creatures that share our precious and unique lives with us, we make a desperate plea on our knees, with our heads bowed and our hearts in our hands.

Do not expect the impossible from your man. Do not expect him to always make you happy, or to light up your existence every day, because it's only your responsibility! Alas, our superpower has dried up over time.

If you feel dissatisfied, if you're not doing well, if you're unhappy (it's only natural) , don't blame your man and don't say that he's the reason for everything that goes wrong, because that would not be true. The problem is inside you, as well as the solution. Don't look for a scapegoat.

You can only find balance inside yourself and without anyone's help, let alone your man's, with all his limitations and flaws!

We don't want you to arrive at the age of forty and be unhappy, thinking that you've married the wrong person and 'ruined' your life. It would be the same with anyone else: your life would be 'ruined' anyway due to an inevitable lack of dreams and heightened loving emotions. This is normal and happens to everyone and it needs to be understood and accepted.

The world is full of dreams and passion; you have to look for and find them in your life, within you and without anyone's help.

Do you choose family, stability, a safe haven? Then be content with what you have, appreciate and value it. You have to look for and find everything else inside and outside of you.

Are you unable to do that? Do you think it's humanly impossible? Isn't it enough to feel good and live happily? Do you miss love terribly?

The family, as we conceive it, is not sustainable and will, inevitably, fall apart.

And all of this for what? For a giddy game? Are you sure it's worth it? You might destroy the second most important thing in your life for something in the fourth or fifth place. Please, don't do it!

Of course, the stones also know that a new romantic fling would make you feel good, improve your life and catapult you sky high. There's no better anti-depressant on the market, indeed, but we already know that the beneficial effects would not last, and everything would inevitably return as before because love always evolves into family over time.

And you think that the only obnoxious and insurmountable obstacle in the world that prevents you from reaching this magnificent El Dorado is exactly your lifetime partner. I'm sure you hate them with all your heart!

§ Sorry, but what should I do when I am in so much pain? Should I renounce love and its beneficial healing effects? Why can't I relive my wonderful and healthy adolescent emotions? Why can't I play again? Nature told me that I can, or rather, that I should – green light! – go where my heart leads me and with my head held high.

Why should I give it up, then? Are there no viable alternatives?

The viable alternative, which is also the solution to our problems, has already been discussed: it's the option to freely and legally follow the first list, the physiological one, that enables us to live well and be complete in every way. In order to do so, however, we would need to change the current laws that regulate our relationships.

This would be the winning choice and the best for everyone, as it would make us feel good and allow us to live as a couple, and by extension our own lives, in a more natural and physiological way.

And if you think that it's too difficult to change the laws globally right now, nothing prevents you from changing them locally, on a small scale. Big changes start small.

§ But how? Are the rules we have proudly created and maintained through the millennia of human history wrong, then? Do they significantly clash with our natural and ancestral programming?

Are they against universal human needs and thus hurt us in the end? Have we shot ourselves in the foot? I've never thought about it before. Are we just finding out about it now?

Well, not now … It was under everyone's nose and has always been clear, but evidently the problem has never been addressed in a serious and efficient manner.

It is enough to know that in Italy, since 2016, the yearly number of separations has matched the yearly number of marriages. This figure demonstrates that we really do have a small problem in relation to the couple. Do we want to keep living this way? Or do we want to do something about it?

Admittedly, this problem is not confined to Italy (indeed, it is universal, right now) and thus concerns every couple – misery loves company, after all – but that doesn't mean we shouldn't still try and change the laws with the aim of finding the winning formula that can accommodate our scale of values, and allow our peaceful coexistence for the rest of our lives.

Regardless of the choices we make, the mere fact that we are talking about the problem and seeking possible solutions from different points of view, is itself a step forward.

This approach allows us to live our lives and our relationships in a lighter and more natural and peaceful way. It's already a good solution, and doesn't create too much upheaval. We could even stop here.

However, I still advise everyone to keep going, continue the journey of change and not limit themselves to merely understand the problem, but also to try to solve it so as to improve their own lives and the lives of future generations.

The road has been laid and the way forward is clear. Go forward, fearless heroes, and continue your courageous journey and your cultural and social revolution. Keep moving, proud, strong and pure; follow the road and reach the final victory. You're heroes!

For the time being, I will limit myself to observing and collecting data, but I'm also rooting for you with trumpets, banners and flags. Let's see what happens.

Especially since – I have just thought of it – I haven't said anything to my wife yet…

… I'll tell her tomorrow!

My dear…

Your eyes are drops of dew

Your hair is crops of golden wheat

Your smile is love and joy

And your words are music and poetry…

My dear…

You are just a cane

and I'm still limping along…

Conclusions about Mood

Our behaviour and our actions are guided by our mood. It might not be evident but it's true: we all are mood-guided, mood-harassed and fortunately mood-rewarded.

Human suffering is physiological, normal, natural, certain, necessary, and often appears without any associated objective cause that can justify it. In fact, we can feel bad even without any apparent reason, and this may lead us to believe that something is wrong with us or with the world around us, but often that is not the case. Suffering is an entirely physiological condition, and it is the same for everyone.

Human beings, in a state of physical or mental rest, naturally tend toward this state of suffering. This is the mechanism that nature has selected to compel us to act, physically or mentally, in order to return to a state of well-being and to be useful and productive for the human species.

Therefore, we should not insist on searching for a cause for this suffering; it is unnecessary, a waste of time and resources. Instead, we should simply act if we want to feel better, and follow the list: socialize, think, plan, create, work, help, solve problems, explore, etc.

.

Mood might be the most important and fundamental function of our body, and it really does affect us. It probably involves many more areas than what we think: indeed, our feelings and emotions could be attributed solely to our mood function, being a nuance or a by-product of it. Thus, they might not even exist as functions in their own right, as we usually think of them.

A little like time: it doesn't exist in nature nor does it move or float in the air as we usually think, because the universe doesn't need time; the only things it needs are space, matter, and energy.

We humans really need time to order to our lives and study physical phenomena though, and for this reason we invented it as a result of the observation and comparison of multiple cyclical physical phenomena.

Since time doesn't exist, we can't measure it and there is no instrument that is designed for this specific purpose, but only instruments or actions that determine, establish or create it, like pendulums, clocks or the clapping of hands.

Similarly, feelings and emotions don't exist on their own, in their own right, because they are too complex and useless for Nature; they are just our imaginative and fantastic interpretation of a phenomenon that is simpler, more practical and more economical in biological and evolutionary terms.

Why should Nature create so many apparently complex functions to regulate our behaviour when it could just use a much simpler one? That is the reason why any attempt to explain and define our emotions is difficult and vague. Of course, this is only a theory.

The mood function can vary from person to person: we are not all the same, and we do not all run on the same "program." But it can also vary depending on **geographical location** — not all places are the same. In fact, we can quite safely say that people born in warm countries, on average, tend to feel better and be happier than people born in cold countries: someone born in the Caribbean is, on average, happier than someone born in Sweden. The reason for this inequality lies precisely in climatic differences, which have the effect of altering the demands of life and survival in these countries. In warm countries, in fact, for 365 days a year there is no need to protect oneself from the cold, and food is, more or less, naturally available. As a result, survival does not require much effort: there is no need to push oneself too hard, no strong need to act, work, build, and so on. Consequently, there is also no need for a powerful driving force compelling people to do these things.
This is very different from cold countries, where for many months of the year the climate is harsh: shelter must be found, food is not naturally available, and therefore the demands of survival are quite different.

One must work, commit, build, cultivate, raise livestock, and so on, if one wants to survive in such a hostile environment. The driving force that makes us do these things is always the same: our mood, the need to try to avoid our physiological suffering, our pain. And to do so, we must obviously act, applying the list, in this case, the "survival" list. In warm countries, suffering is on average reduced and not needed to a great extent, whereas in cold countries it is absolutely necessary — therefore very much present, tormenting people, but also indispensable for survival in such inhospitable environments.

Even simple life **problems** must generate suffering and lower our mood (e.g. financial problems), so that we are forced to solve them if we want to feel well again. In fact, if a problem did not lead to a decrease in our mood, if it did not make us feel bad, we would do nothing to try to solve it, we would not feel the need to, and it would remain unchanged, and both the world and our lives would fall apart.

Grief is also a physiological mechanism that causes a sharp and lasting drop in our mood, triggered by the loss or separation from someone we care about. Grief serves the purpose of keeping us united and encouraging us to take care of the people we love: in fact, we stay with them and care for them precisely to avoid the suffering of grief.

Examples include the (often obsessive and

constant) protection of children by parents, or the care of elderly parents by their children, situations that can sometimes lead to senseless and irrational therapeutic obstinacy, driven by a selfish refusal of the suffering of grief: in order not to suffer my own grief, I end up unnecessarily making my loved one suffer! This is not right, because it is certainly not an act of love.

Mood varies from person to person because it is the result of natural selection, but a generally lower mood (without exaggeration) can also give a person greater chances to emerge, stand out, and "rise above" others, as seen in artists, poets, scientists, musicians, writers, entrepreneurs, and so on, out of survival necessity: being pushed to act more than others in order to return to a state of well-being.

However, if excessive, this condition can also risk destroying the person, which unfortunately sometimes happens. Those who are generally well tend to be more stable and calm, and are less likely to develop these kinds of creative drives or pressures.

Let's talk about mood again and ask ourselves a fundamental question: what will our mood be like at the end of our lives, existence, journey and everything? What will the final bill, the algebraic sum, be? Will it be positive or negative? Will we have been happier or sadder? Will we have been fortunate or unfortunate?

§ Well, I don't know. We can't know in advance. It will depend on our lives, our experiences, our lifestyle, our luck or lack thereof, and much more. It's difficult to predict.

Of course, I hope my final balance sheet will be positive!

It won't be, though, because our compass doesn't work that way. On average (we are not all the same) and excluding any major upsets, the final balance will be neither positive nor negative, because our compass never gives us anything for nothing, for better or for worse. Positive and negative moods compensate each other in the end and none of them can prevail in the long run.

That's exactly what Nature intended in order to make the human machine work properly. Other options, like the possibility of always being happy, wouldn't have been possible. Alas, it didn't manage to survive natural selection.

Being sad, too, isn't advantageous for the human species either, but all biological rules depend on randomness and natural selection, in short the Gaussian distribution. Thus, pathological sadness happens to someone.

Our graph shows that in the long run, the sum of positive areas will equal the sum of the negative areas, whatever our behaviour or the environment, where we live, is.

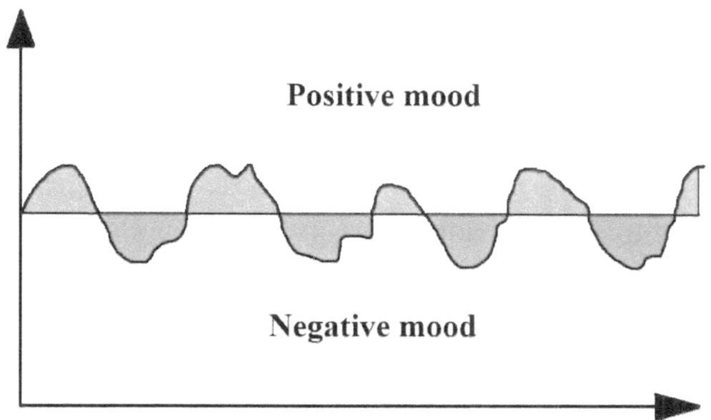

The final balance will always be zero for any labourer, employee, entrepreneur or lawyer. It will always be zero for any millionaire, famous actor or Prince Joe Public.

We are all the same because our mood answers to no one. In a way, mood is democratic, fair and socially just, and it gives back no change in the end.

§ If that's true, we are ruined! How can we live well if the result is always zero? Why should we go to all this trouble if nothing changes? How can I improve my life if living well is the same as living badly?

It isn't true that we are ruined, because despite the result we can still live well or badly; it depends on us, our behaviour and our lifestyle.

Mood must be wide-ranging and dynamic; in the end, it's the curve area that makes the difference. The integral mathematical function really matters, as well as the intensity and rate of positive spikes which are the ones that ultimately make our lives shine, light them up, and that we are very good at remembering, associating, and storing in our memory.

If you want to live well, you should prevent your mood curve from flattening, and that's fundamental, but you also need coherence and coordination between your mood and your real life. When the negative phases of mood are associated with real, concrete and physiological motivations, they hurt less and better intensify the subsequent positive phases.

'Those who do not suffer, do not enjoy life.

Those who suffer in a bad way, suffer more and enjoy life less.

Those who suffer in a good way, suffer less and enjoy life more.'

Often the negative phases that we feel and experience nowadays are artificial and psychological; they are malevolent creatures just like stress and frenzy and the useless needs and worries that afflict our everyday lives.

They don't really work with our natural, ancestral mood mechanism because they are not natural and physiological as they should be and for this reason, they are ineffective in making our mood dynamic.

Well-being exists in our society, that's undeniable, but it's only material well-being that doesn't effectively reflect in the global well-being of the individual: we finally live in a world of well-being, but we ourselves are no longer well', it seems like a paradox.

If we want to maintain this lifestyle, with its luxuries and comforts, we should also accept that our mood curve will tend to flatten and that suffering will always be present, even if unjustified and in a reduced form. If you want to make your mood dynamic, you need negative phases that are real, concrete and physiological.

Have you ever wondered why a film is deemed good and worth watching?

§ Because it tells a good story.

What's a good story, though?

§ A story that people like. An interesting story, that makes us feel good, stimulates our feelings and emotions and… How should I know?

Yes, it makes us feel good, but why? Because it makes our mood dynamic, with moments of 'virtual' suffering and pleasure that alternate with each other, amplifying the ups and downs and thus the area of the whole curve.

A bad film is bad because it does not have a good effect on our mood and typically leaves it flat. Moreover, if we need to wipe away our tears while watching a film, then we'll feel good after leaving the cinema: it's the *rebound* effect on our mood of the negative phases we were immersed in and which we experienced virtually. After the film, we will remember how good we felt, and recommend it to everyone.

Just ask yourself the reason why millions of people go jogging, go cycling, go to the gym, work hard, sweat, even overdo it, doing things that have no purpose!

§ What do you mean by 'no purpose'? Aren't they good for your health and how you look.

Well, I'm not sure that they are good for your body; anyway, that's not the real reason.

You don't do those activities because they are good for you, but because they make you feel good, which is something else. You do them because they increase your mood and the well-being they produce follows the physical activity, as a direct consequence of the action itself (because I act and move) and of the suffering that we involuntarily 'produce' and 'consume' during the whole 'ordeal'.

It is exactly this suffering, well-justified and concrete, physical and psychological, that due to this *rebound* effect gives us well-being, while strongly preventing the flattening of our mood curve.

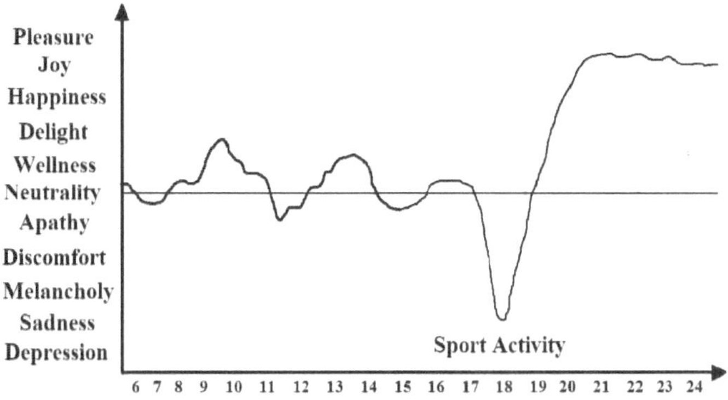

I invite everyone to get out regularly to do some good physical activity that requires effort, commitment and sweat. This way, we recreate both the physical and psychological healthy 'suffering' we all need (and which may be missing in our lives); this can then be associated with our mood's negative emotions. It's a bit as if we voluntarily and concretely 'consume' inevitable suffering, whenever we want to, in order to improve the dynamic of our mood.

Those who do not suffer cannot enjoy life. It's mathematical and inevitable. Unfortunately, many of us do anything to avoid this kind of healthy and physiological suffering, shooting ourselves in the foot in the process.

Also, if we want to feel good, we also need to regularly engage in the many positive, natural activities that increase our mood. Do you remember them? Did you write them on your list? Are you following them?

You need to do a bit of everything with the right balance, diversifying your interests as much as possible, without focusing only on one of them, even if it seems the best and most appealing, like food or love!

Alas, right now we have little time to devote ourselves wholeheartedly to our lists, because we are too busy working and earning the money we need to do useless and superfluous stuff that hurts us and the environment, and that doesn't even make us happy in the end... how foolish we are

§ Okay, I accept it. What can we do to get out of the stalemate we have got into? It's difficult to change universally accepted social norms, I suppose. In any case, how can we change our lives for the better if we risk changing our lives for the worse in this precise moment?

The simplest solution would be to apply the '**rule of 50%**' to our lives, halving its insane speed: we should halve the time we spend working, our consumption, our needs, our movements, our demands. We should halve everything, doubling our free time and healthily and sustainably devoting it to ourselves, others and the environment in which we live.

Of course, we'll have to make some concessions. Will they really be concessions, though? Of course, we will all be materially poorer, although poorer in what way? Won't we only have got rid of all the luxuries, as well as other superfluous and useless things?

The sure thing is that we will all be healthier, more beautiful, and richer in our hearts, having the right amount of time and space to express our spirituality and humanity once again.

If we all made these healthy changes to our lives right now, we would all be more peaceful, happier and more satisfied, and live physically and psychically healthy lives in a healthy, beautiful and sustainable environment.

Therefore, let's get cracking and hit the brakes. Let's slow down, and begin, with utmost respect for everything and everyone, to enjoy our unique, short…

… and magnificent Existence!